The Freedom of Faith-Based Organizations to Staff on a Religious Basis

The Freedom of Faith-Based Organizations to Staff on a Religious Basis

Carl H. Esbeck
Stanley W. Carlson-Thies
Ronald J. Sider

The Center for Public Justice
Washington, DC

ISBN: 0-936456-04-3
Library of Congress Control Number: 2004113255

Published by The Center for Public Justice, Washington, DC

Distributed by Evangelicals for Social Action, Wynnewood, PA

Additional copies of book can be ordered for $10.00 plus postage* from:

Evangelicals for Social Action
10 East Lancaster Avenue
Wynnewood, PA 19096
1-800-650-6600
www.esa-online.org

* PA residents add 6% sales tax

An Adobe® Reader® PDF version of this book can be downloaded without
charge at these websites:

The Center for Public Justice   <http://www.cpjustice.org>
Evangelicals for Social Action   <http://www.esa-online.org>
The Christian Legal Society   <http://www.clsnet.org>

Table of Contents

Executive Summary

In the ongoing debate over the faith-based initiative to expand the role of community-serving religious groups, opponents claim that religious charities, when accepting funding from the government to provide services to distressed communities and the poor, have thereby forfeited their freedom to employ staff of like-minded faith. This is not the case. Under section 702(a) of the Civil Rights Act of 1964, religious organizations are free to take religion into account when selecting their employees. Section 702(a) is not waived by religious organizations merely because they receive federal funding to conduct their social-service activities, as every court to pass on the question has acknowledged.

It is also a mistake to claim, as some opponents of the initiative do, that religious staffing by a faith-based charity violates the Establishment Clause of the First Amendment. It is elementary that the Bill of Rights, including the Establishment Clause, was adopted to restrain only government, not the independent sector. If a particular social-service provider has an employment policy rooted in its religious mission, the policy is solely that of the provider. Receipt of a government grant or contract does not change the independent nature of that decision. Because a provider's employment decisions are wholly independent of the government, the Establishment Clause is not even implicated. In a unanimous decision handed down in

1987, the U.S. Supreme Court agreed, observing that the religious staffing decisions of a church-operated facility are not attributable to the government.

Spurious claims have also been made that the faith-based initiative will result in increased job discrimination against women and those with alternative lifestyles. These speculations are misguided. The initiative does not alter the status quo when it comes to federal civil rights coverage of employment discrimination based on sex or lifestyle. Nor is there any change with respect to discrimination on the basis of race, color, national origin, age, or disability.

Most legislation implementing federal social-service programs imposes no requirements—other than those already imposed by the 1964 Civil Rights Act—concerning the employment practices of independent-sector providers that participate in the programs. However, some federal programs do have embedded in their implementing legislation a requirement that all grant recipients agree not to discriminate in employment on various bases, including religion. When faced with such a requirement, religious charities may turn to the Religious Freedom Restoration Act of 1993 (RFRA) for protection. RFRA is a federal civil rights law that broadly relieves religious organizations of burdens on their religious practices imposed by otherwise applicable federal law. A prohibition on religious staffing clearly falls into this category. It is no answer to argue, as opponents of the faith-based initiative do, that a restriction on religious staffing imposes no burden on religion because a faith-based charity can avoid the burden simply by turning down the federal funding. That makes no sense. Religious providers should not be put to the cruel choice of either forgoing grant funding or recanting on a matter of religious conscience. Section 7 of RFRA expressly contemplates that a "denial of government funding" because of a grant recipient's religious practice (here, staffing with those of like-minded faith) is a burden that triggers RFRA protection.

When the federal government itself awards monies directly to a social-service provider, it is either by way of a "discretionary" grant authorized by statute or an "ear-marked" grant set out in a congressional appropriations bill. Federal law alone governs the legal responsibilities that go with such grant awards, thus—as indicated above—the freedom to staff on a religious basis is not restricted (except in those instances where a program's statute has an embedded restriction). However, more commonly, the federal monies go first to a state or local government and only thereafter are awarded to independent-sector providers. In these circumstances, the application of state and local laws must also be considered.

It is common for state and local governments, as they administer grant monies, to have "procurement" laws (also called "purchasing" or "contracting" laws) that bind independent-sector recipients of these monies—including monies that first originated with the federal government. These procurement laws generally concern the proper accounting of program funds. However, procurement laws in some state and local jurisdictions prohibit employment discrimination on various bases, including religion. When a religious charity receives federal funds by way of such a state or local government, then the question arises whether the charity has possibly lost—because of the operation of an applicable procurement law—the freedom to staff on a religious basis.

If the federal funds are subject to the rules of Charitable Choice, then the religious charity's freedom to staff on a religious basis is retained. Charitable Choice was adopted by Congress with the understanding that it protects religious staffing rights. It does so by overriding state and local procurement laws that would undermine the essential religious character of faith-based organizations. Congress first adopted Charitable Choice in 1996 in an effort to encourage greater participation by faith-based providers in welfare programming. Without safeguards like those in Charitable Choice, many religious charities were simply unwilling to risk becoming entangled in the regulatory "strings" that come with government funding.

If the federal funds are not subject to Charitable Choice, then some state and local authorities argue that their procurement laws presumptively block a faith-based provider's religious staffing freedom. We say "presumptively" because religious charities will surely raise their right not to be subject to regulatory "strings" that discriminate against their full and equal exercise of First Amendment freedoms. This claim was greatly bolstered by federal regulations recently promulgated pursuant to Executive Order 13279 (Dec. 12, 2002), which expressly provide for the autonomy of participating faith-based service providers. It is uncertain how the courts will resolve this clash between a faith-based organization's claim of freedom to staff on a religious basis and a state's professed power to put conditions on the use of funds that originated with the federal government.

Where Charitable Choice is not applicable, religious charities are well advised to exercise more care when applying to a state or local government for federal funds. Grant applicants should determine whether the jurisdiction awarding the grant has an employment nondiscrimination procurement law and whether the authorities intend to enforce it so as to prohibit faith-based organizations from hiring on the basis of religion.

It is wrong for government to shift the burden of regulatory uncertainty and costly litigation onto religious charities. Congress should act to remove any remaining doubt that religious staffing rights take precedent over these restrictive state and local procurement rules. Federal funds should be governed by federal rules regardless of the state, county, or city where the federal programs operate. Nationwide legal uniformity will hasten the development of a more effective social safety net, and the greater regulatory simplicity for grant applicants will increase their efficiency and save the government money. The continued threat of restrictive procurement rules in some jurisdictions only operates to keep religious providers from expanding their works of compassion, and that hurts the poor and needy.

To review, the logic of the current state of the law is as follows:

- Section 702(a) of the Civil Rights Act of 1964 expressly acknowledges the freedom of religious organizations to staff with those of like-minded faith, and this freedom is neither waived nor rendered unconstitutional when the organization receives federal funds.

- Safeguarding the freedom of religious organizations to staff on a religious basis does not increase unlawful job discrimination for women or those with alternative lifestyles.

- The underlying legislation that implements most federal social-service programs has no additional restrictions concerning the employment practices of independent-sector providers receiving federal grants. However, a minority of federal programs do have such restrictions. Where such program grants are involved, a religious organization may turn to RFRA to maintain its freedom to staff on a religious basis.

- The situation is more complex when federal funds flow first to state or local governments before being awarded to independent-sector providers. Such jurisdictions typically have procurement laws, and sometimes these laws prohibit employment discrimination on various bases, including religion. If the federal funds originated with a program subject to Charitable Choice, then a religious service provider retains its essential religious character including the ability to hire consistent with its faith.

- If Charitable Choice is not applicable, then where state and local procurement rules prohibit hiring in a manner that takes faith into account, there is a conflict of two laws. Religious charities will surely raise their First Amendment freedoms, as well as rely on the autonomy language in regulations promulgated under Executive Order 13279. It is presently unclear how this clash between restrictive procurement laws and a religious charity's federal rights and defenses will be resolved.

1 The Faith-Based Initiative and the Controversy over Religious Staffing

The movement to encourage greater participation by faith-based organizations in government-funded social-service programs began in earnest with the adoption of the Charitable Choice rules as part of the federal welfare reform act signed into law by President Bill Clinton in August 1996.[1] Charitable Choice rules were also included in three

---

The 1996 welfare reform law contained a little-known provision called Charitable Choice. It says, simply, that states can enlist faith-based organizations to provide basic welfare services, and help move people from welfare to work.

As long as there is always a secular alternative for anyone who wants one, and as long as no one is required to participate in religious observances as a condition for receiving services, faith-based organizations can provide jobs and job training, counseling and mentoring, food and basic medical care. They can do so with public funds—and without having to alter the religious character that is so often the key to their effectiveness.

I believe we should extend this carefully tailored approach to other vital services where faith-based organizations can play a role—such as drug treatment, homelessness, and youth violence prevention.

—Vice President Al Gore, speaking to The Salvation Army, Atlanta, May 24, 1999.

---

[1]*See* Section 104 of the Personal Responsibility and Work Opportunity Reconciliation Act of 1996, Pub. L. No. 104-193, 110 Stat. 2105 (1996) (codified at 42 U.S.C § 604a); *reprinted in* Appendix 3.

additional bills approved by President Clinton before he left office. In the 2000 presidential race the rules were endorsed not only by Republican candidate George W. Bush but also by his Democratic opponent, Vice President Al Gore.

Government funding of religious charities to provide a range of social services did not, of course, begin with the 1996 welfare reform law. For years federal, state, and local governments have included church-related and religiously affiliated groups among the providers whose services they financially support. Catholic Charities, Lutheran Services, Jewish Federations, and the Salvation Army are but the most prominent of the religiously inspired organizations that have long collaborated with government. However, a strict separationist interpretation of the First Amendment rendered partnerships between government and religious providers always somewhat questionable and vulnerable to legal or political challenge.[2]

The Charitable Choice rules, as well as the faith-based initiative launched by George W. Bush at the start of his presidency, are designed to reduce the uncertainty that has clouded this relationship. Two distinct decades-old trends undergird these efforts to create more extensive and better-grounded collaborations between government programs and faith-based providers of social services. One trend is the search for more effective responses to poverty and other social problems by making the delivery of social services more collaborative than in the past. The hope is that in this way government can gain the special strengths of faith-based and community-based providers that are situated in close proximity to the

---

[2] Stephen V. Monsma, *When Sacred and Secular Mix: Religious Nonprofit Organizations and Public Money* (1996). Such uncertainty apparently is one reason why many big foundations and corporations are reluctant to support faith-based service programs. "In 1998, only some 2 percent of the billions of dollars given by the nation's 1,000 largest foundations went to religiously affiliated institutions . . . . [S]ix of the country's ten largest businesses . . . 'ban or restrict' donations to religious groups; AT&T's contributions, for instance, are exclusively reserved, as its website announces, for organizations that are 'nonsectarian and nondenominational.'" Leslie Lenkowsky, *Funding the Faithful: Why Bush is Right*, Commentary (June 1, 2001).

needy, motivated by compassion, trusted by those who require help, and respectful of deeply held values.

The second trend is the shift in First Amendment interpretation away from no-aid strict separationism and toward the concept of equal treatment or neutrality. From a neutrality perspective, the government's obligation is not to choose the secular over the religious. Rather, its duty is to deal evenhandedly with all providers seeking support, whether they are secular, church-affiliated, or highly religious, focusing solely on a provider's capability to deliver the program services effectively and efficiently. This change in interpretive framework, manifest in U.S. Supreme Court cases, led directly to the developments enabling Charitable Choice and the faith-based initiative.[3]

One of the goals of the new initiative is to increase the visibility of the faith-based and community-based groups that are "neighborhood healers": houses of worship, neighborhood groups, and small nonprofits that play a vital role in responding to human needs and upholding neglected communities. Another goal is to stimulate greater private giving, both individual and corporate, to these and other charities.[4]

---

[3] For the link with Charitable Choice, *see* Carl H. Esbeck, *The Neutral Treatment of Religion and Faith-Based Social Service Providers: Charitable Choice and Its Critics in* WELFARE REFORM AND FAITH-BASED ORGANIZATIONS 173-217 (Derek Davis and Barry Hankins, eds., 1999); and Carl H. Esbeck, *A Constitutional Case for Governmental Cooperation with Faith-Based Social Service Providers*, 46 Emory Law Journal 1-41 (Winter, 1997). For the link with the Bush Administration's faith-based initiative, see White House Office of Faith-Based and Community Initiatives, Executive Office of the President, *Unlevel Playing Field: Barriers to Participation by Faith-Based and Community Organizations in Federal Social Service Programs*, 10-13 (August, 2001); President George W. Bush, *Rallying the Armies of Compassion: Message from the President of the United States Transmitting a Report to Support the Heroic Works of Faith-Based and Community Groups Across America*, H.R. Doc. No. 107-36, 107th Cong., 1st Sess. 9 (2001); and the notice of the final rule for *Charitable Choice Provisions Applicable to the Temporary Assistance for Needy Families Program*, 68 Fed. Reg. 56451, 56456 (Sept. 30, 2003), *excerpted in* Appendix 4.

[4] For a discussion of the several goals of the faith-based initiative, see President George W. Bush, *Rallying the Armies of Compassion* (2001). Restoration of the deductibility of charitable contributions by non-itemizing federal taxpayers and other measures to promote greater private giving have been central elements of "faith-based legislation" proposed in Congress during the Bush Administration. See, e.g., H.R. 7, the Community Solutions Act, which was passed by the House in July, 2001, but, due to controversy over its expansion of Charitable Choice, was not taken up by the Senate; the CARE Act of 2003 (S. 476), passed by the Senate in April 2003; and the House companion bill to the CARE Act, the Charitable Giving Act of 2003 (H.R. 7), passed by the House in September, 2003.

However, the most prominent—and most contentious—goal has been the effort to reform federal policies and practices to create an equal opportunity for faith-based providers to receive financial support. Contrary to the critics, the aim is not government favoritism for religious providers, but rather a level playing field in government funding policies. Only in this manner can all providers, religious or not, be judged on the merits of their proposals and programs, and not on whether religion has been safely confined to the margins of civil society.

Four fundamental principles undergird Charitable Choice and the faith-based initiative's effort to reform the way the federal government financially supports social-service providers:[5]

- Faith-based providers are eligible to compete for government funding on the same basis as other independent-sector social-service providers, being neither favored nor penalized because of their religious character. The government's goal is to select the best provider. There is no guarantee that faith-based providers will receive funding, only that they have an equal opportunity to compete.

- The terms of the government funding must be free of requirements that undermine the very religious character that inspires and animates faith-based organizations. Providers should not find it necessary either to secularize themselves or to take themselves out of the competition. Safeguarding a provider's freedom to select employees dedicated to their faith-based mission is an essential element of this protection of institutional integrity.

---

[5]For these principles in the context of Charitable Choice, *see* Stanley W. Carlson-Thies and Carl H. Esbeck, *A Guide to Charitable Choice: The Rules of Section 104 of the 1996 Federal Welfare Law Governing State Cooperation with Faith-based Social-Service Providers* (1997) *available at* <www.cpjustice.org/charitablechoice/guide/>; and Stanley W. Carlson-Thies, *Charitable Choice for Welfare and Community Services: An Implementation Guide for State, Local, and Federal Officials* (2000) *available at* <http://www.cpjustice.org/stories/storyReader$371>.

For the principles of the Bush faith-based initiative, see *Equal Protection of the Laws for Faith-Based and Community Organizations,* Executive Order 13279, 67 Fed. Reg. 77141 (Dec. 12, 2002), *reprinted in* Appendix 6; and White House Office of Faith-Based and Community Initiatives, Executive Office of the President, *Guidance to Faith-Based and Community Organizations on Partnering with the Federal*

- Government grants and other direct assistance may not be taken from the intended program services and diverted to inherently religious activities such as religious instruction, proselytizing, or worship.[6] Such activities can be offered if separated by time or location from the government-funded program.

- The individual religious liberty of the beneficiaries receiving assistance from a faith-based provider is protected by ensuring that beneficiaries are not required to take part in unwanted religious activities, but can receive services free from religious coercion.

These four principles represent a clarification of the appropriate rules for the government's financial collaboration with religious social-service providers, a clarification consistent with the Supreme Court's shift away from strict separationism and toward neutrality or equal treatment. These principles are also valuable because they enable government officials to select from the entire range of effective providers, and because they enlarge the options for the beneficiaries qualifying for assistance—many of whom prefer to be served by a religious provider.

A. The Charge of Violating the Separation of Church and State

Opponents, in sharp contrast, have argued that the concept of neutrality or equal treatment of faith-based with secular providers violates the separation of church and state. That objection has gained little traction on

---

Government (Dec. 12, 2002).

[6]Following a series of U.S. Supreme Court rulings, when the funding is "indirect" rather than "direct"— that is, when the funds arrive at the faith-based provider not because of a government official's decision, but due to the choice of the beneficiary (e.g., through a certificate such as is used for most federally funded child care)—then inherently religious elements need not be separated out from the government-funded services. Of course, the secular purpose of the funding must still be met, e.g., the provision of child care, ensuring a transition from welfare to work, drug abuse counseling, and so on. *See Zelman v. Simmons-Harris*, 536 U.S. 639 (2002) (upholding vouchers for K-12 religious schools); *Zobrest v. Catalina Foothills Sch. Dist.*, 509 U.S. 1 (1993) (upholding the provision of special education services at religious school); *Witters v. Washington Dep't of Servs. for the Blind*, 474 U.S. 481 (1986) (upholding student's use of vocational training assistance at religious college to seek degree in pastoral studies); *Mueller v. Allen*, 463 U.S. 388 (1983) (upholding income tax deduction for educational expenses of

THE FREEDOM OF FAITH-BASED ORGANIZATIONS TO STAFF ON A RELIGIOUS BASIS

the floor of Congress, in popular opinion, or in the federal courts.[7] Few are convinced that an organization should be barred from competing for government funds merely because it identifies its core mission as faith-centered or because part of the staff's motivation for serving is religious faith. Nor does having religious words in an organization's name or religious symbols on the premises seem to most people sufficient reason to disqualify an otherwise eligible organization from receiving government support for its social-service programs.

Government officials, at least those close to the front lines where the programs are actually implemented, began to realize that they were defeating their own secular objectives of reducing human needs and strengthening communities when they excluded some of the most trusted and well-positioned charities. Too often the policy elite, who typically are far removed from blighted neighborhoods, have spurned the involvement of religious providers simply because these charities are "too religious." But the goal of public social programs is to reduce poverty, revitalize low-income communities, and empower families and individuals to become more fully self-sufficient. The accomplishment of these vital goals calls for a religion-neutral rule that asks service providers not, "How religious are you?" but, "Can you do the job?" and, "Will you operate within the rules?"

---

parents enrolling child in K-12 religious school).

[7]The Supreme Court has upheld as constitutional direct assistance to independent-sector providers, including religious providers, and it makes no difference whether the recipient organization was minimally or highly religious. *See Mitchell v. Helms*, 530 U.S. 793 (2000) (sustaining K-12 educational assistance). However, it is imperative that the aid be used only for the designated educational or welfare services—not diverted to inherently religious activities. *Id.* at 836-67 (O'Connor, J., concurring in the judgment). So long as there is no diversion, then it does not matter whether the provider is "pervasively sectarian" or otherwise highly religious. For example, in *Mitchell* the educational providers receiving the assistance were K-12 religious schools. This was a rejection of prior case law such as *Bowen v. Kendrick*, 487 U.S. 589 (1988), insofar as the older cases did not permit direct aid to "pervasively sectarian" organizations.

For a fuller discussion of *Mitchell*, see Testimony by Carl H. Esbeck, Senior Counsel to the Deputy Attorney General; before the House Subcomm. on the Constitution, Comm. on the Judiciary, June 7, 2001, *reprinted in* 2 Notre Dame Journal of Law, Ethics & Public Policy 567-86 (2002); David M. Ackerman, *Public Aid to Faith-Based Organizations (Charitable Choice) in the 107th Congress: Background and Selected Legal Issues*, Congressional Research Service Report for Congress, order code RL31043, 35-45 (Aug. 19, 2003).

Americans are a religious people, and the First Amendment commits the government to minimizing where possible its interference with religious belief and practice. A rule forbidding government funding of those religiously affiliated charities that take their faith most seriously might be plausible if there is little overlap between the charity's sphere of activity and the policy objectives of government programs. But our modern active government with its extensive social-service system has no such rigid division. Instead, government supplies the great bulk of the social services and does so by funding independent-sector providers. Given that government may permissibly follow a rule of noninterference with religious belief and practice, and given the modern state's heavy involvement in the provision of social services through independent providers, then a rule of neutrality best delivers the needed services while minimizing the influence of the government on religious choices. As law professor Douglas Laycock observed in testimony before Congress:

> [B]uying [social services] without regard to religion . . . minimizes government's influence on religious choices and commitments. If government buys without regard to religion, no one has to change their religious behavior to do business with the government. This is the key concept of charitable choice. It is a good concept. Despite the conventional wisdom of many separationists, funding everyone equally separates private religious choice from government influence more effectively than funding only secular providers.[8]

A religion-blind distribution of government aid promotes greater religious choice and desirable noninterference, and thereby a separation of the administrative spheres of church and state. Neutral treatment also means that the religious choices of the poor and needy are less influenced by how the government does its business.

---

[8]*The Constitutional Role of Faith-Based Organizations in Competitions for Federal Social Service Funds*, Testimony by Douglas Laycock, Professor of Law, Univ. of Texas at Austin; before the House Subcomm. on the Constitution, Comm. on the Judiciary, 107th Cong., June 7, 2001, 21, *available at* <http://www.house.gov/judiciary/72981.pdf>.

B. The Charge of Government-Funded Discrimination

Frustrated when the older arguments for strict separationism could not reverse the growing appeal of the faith-based initiative, opponents retooled their rhetoric. This thrust began in great earnest in January 2001 just as the 107th Congress was getting underway and President Bush was establishing the White House Office of Faith-Based and Community Initiatives. The new emphasis was on disparaging the faith-based initiative as a form of "government-funded discrimination"—a false characterization of the fact that religious providers often hire those of like-minded faith. The accusation, while seriously misleading, had an immediate impact on the public policy debate. If religious staffing rights could be pitched as "job discrimination," in violation of people's "civil rights," few politicians wanted to line up on the wrong side of a skirmish over civil rights.

Organizations with a clear sense of mission—whether religious or not—quite naturally work hard to select and maintain a staff that shares their vision. Because of their religious character, many faith-based organizations understandably do select some or all of their staff on a religious basis.[9] Yet choosing employees of like-minded faith—good management practice for many religious organizations hoping to sustain their vision—was transformed by opponents of the faith-based initiative into "job discrimination," a seemingly bigoted practice, and one made worse if abetted by government funding. Moreover, the opponents did not stop with rhetoric but additionally claimed that religious hiring practices—when federal social-service funds are added to the mix—are both contrary to federal civil rights legislation and violate the Establishment Clause.

This is a fundamentally incorrect representation of the law.

The purpose of this monograph is to set forth the applicable legislative and constitutional law and the rationale that undergirds it, as well as the

---

[9] In addition to Chapters 2 and 5, below, *see* Charles L. Glenn, *The Ambiguous Embrace: Government and Faith-Based Schools and Social Agencies,* ch. 6 (2000) (discussing the importance of religious staffing to many faith-based organizations).

important public policy reasons that support religious staffing by faith-based providers. We do not, of course, claim that faith-based social-service providers are immune from the rule of law or regulatory rules. We believe, rather, that they are subject to reasonable restrictions, and that the requirements of accountability do increase when government funds are involved. However, regulatory restraints must stop short of compromising the religious integrity of faith-based organizations. There is no point in a government initiative that welcomes the participation of faith-based providers because of their effective work in serving distressed communities, only to do them harm by legal snares that undermine the religious character that makes them successful. The oft-used term "independent sector" is an oxymoron if government regulations crush the integrity and flatten out the distinctives of its faith-based partners. Such an approach defeats the government's own social-service policy objectives, and will surely end up harming rather than helping the poor.

2   *Religious Staffing: Legislation and the Constitution*

Religious nonprofit organizations that provide social services to the poor and needy do have the freedom under federal civil rights law to staff (hire, promote, discharge) on a basis that takes into account the organization's religious beliefs and practices. Moreover, that freedom is not forfeited simply because such an organization receives federal social-service funds.

To fully explain this staffing freedom, the legal discussion that follows is necessarily detailed and, at points, complex. This is partly because we must deal with both federal and state laws and also with local ordinances. It is partly because we must deal with constitutions, statutes, and regulations, as well as with court cases interpreting all of the foregoing. And it is partly because we must deal with both the general authority of government to regulate for the welfare of society and with the more narrow authority that allows government to attach conditions to the expenditure of public funds.

Hopefully, as we proceed through these layers of detail and complexity, the state of the law and its rationale will logically unfold and become clear. Whether you are an official administering a program or on the staff of a faith-based organization that is contemplating applying for government funds, we encourage you to seek legal counsel with respect to your specific questions and unique situation, and to begin by supplying a copy of this monograph to your lawyer.

A. Religious Staffing and the Federal Civil Rights Act of 1964

The fundamental federal civil rights employment law, Title VII of the Civil Rights Act of 1964,[10] prohibits employment discrimination on the basis of race, color, religion, sex, or national origin. The legislation initially applied only to employers with 25 or more employees. The law was binding on religious organizations—at least, that is, with regard to the prohibition of employment discrimination on the basis of race, color, sex, or national origin. Religion was different. Pursuant to section 702, religious organizations were not subject to claims of religious discrimination brought by employees responsible for "religious activities."[11]

The 1964 act was amended by the Equal Employment Opportunity Act of 1972.[12] The coverage of Title VII was expanded to employers with as few as 15 employees. Most important for present purposes, the text of 702 was broadened in scope to enable religious organizations to take religion into account for all of the organization's employees,[13] whatever their

---

[10] 42 U.S.C. §§ 2000e et seq. See Pub. L. No. 88-352, 78 Stat. 253 (1964).

[11] Section 702 originally read, in relevant part, as follows: "This title shall not apply . . . to a religious corporation, association, or society with respect to the employment of individuals of a particular religion to perform work connected with the carrying on by such corporation, association, or society of its religious activities or to an educational institution with respect to the employment of individuals to perform work connected with the educational activities of such institution." 78 Stat. 255.

[12] Pub. L. No. 92-261, 86 Stat. 103 (1972).

[13] Section 702(a) presently provides, in relevant part, as follows: "This title shall not apply to . . . a religious corporation, association, educational institution, or society with respect to the employment of individuals of a particular religion to perform work connected with the carrying on by such corporation, association, educational institution, or society of its activities." 42 U.S.C. § 2000e-1(a).

activities within the organization, whether "religious" or not.[14]

> Civil Rights Act of 1964, Title VII, Section 702(a), as amended in 1972: "This title shall not apply to . . . a religious corporation, association, educational institution, or society with respect to the employment of individuals of a particular religion to perform work connected with the carrying on by such corporation, association, educational institution, or society of its activities."
> —42 U.S.C. § 2000e-1(a)

The 1972 act broadened 702 out of a concern that government regulators would otherwise be able to interfere with the religious affairs of religious organizations.[15] The congressional sponsors of the amendment to broaden 702 (now designated § 702(a)) were Senators Allen and Ervin. They explained the amendment's purpose in terms of a need to further restrain the government's power in order to keep a proper distance between church and state. Senator Sam Ervin, a Democrat from North Carolina who was widely recognized as an expert on the U.S. Constitution, said of the proposal:

> [T]he amendment would exempt religious corporations, associations, and societies from the application of this act insofar as the right to employ people of any religion they see fit is concerned. . . . In other words, this amendment is to take the political hands of Caesar off the institutions of God, where they have no place to be.[16]

---

[14]In both its original, limited form and in its amended form, the religious staffing freedom of 702(a) does not absolve covered faith-based organizations from the obligation not to discriminate in employment on the bases of race, color, sex, or national origin. Moreover, other federal civil rights laws prohibit employment discrimination, including by religious organizations, on the bases of age and disability, and require equal pay for equal work without regard to the sex of employees. The Age Discrimination in Employment Act, 29 U.S.C. §§ 621-634, prohibits employment discrimination on the basis of age. It applies to employers of 20 or more employees. There is no exemption set forth in the act for religious organizations. The Americans with Disabilities Act, 42 U.S.C. §§ 12101-12213, prohibits discrimination against otherwise qualified individuals with disabilities. The employment protections are found at §§ 12111-12117. The ADA applies to employers of 15 or more employees. The ADA permits religious organizations to staff on a religious basis. *Id.* at § 12113(c). Finally, the Equal Pay Act of 1963, 29 U.S.C. § 206(d), requires equal pay for equal work without regard to sex. It applies to employers who are also subject to the federal minimum wage. There is no statutory exemption for religious organizations.

[15]*See Little v. Wuerl*, 929 F.2d 944, 949-51 (3d Cir. 1991) (giving a brief account of the congressional purpose behind broadening 702(a)).

[16]118 Cong. Rec. 4503 (Feb. 17, 1972) (remarks by Senator Sam Ervin).

For government regulators and, ultimately, the courts to have the power to pry into a religious organization's job descriptions, lines of supervisory authority, allocation of assignments, performance reviews, personnel reprimands, and the like, and to sift n' sort as to the nature and degree of "religious" duties as distinct from "secular" duties for any given job, invites untoward governmental interference with internal religious matters.[17] The Establishment Clause was designed to deregulate the religious sphere and thereby restrain such regulatory interference;[18] hence, Senator Ervin's remark that Caesar is to keep his "political hands off" religious organizations. Accordingly, the government does not have the power to determine which of a faith-based organization's jobs are "secular enough" to be regulated by government and which are "so religious" that they are off-limits. In short, enlarging the scope of 702(a) was about reinforcing our nation's venerable tradition of separating church and state.[19]

In addition to 702(a), Congress acknowledges in 703(e) of Title VII the

---

[17] A long line of Supreme Court cases admonish government, including the courts, to avoid probing into the religious meaning of the words, practices, and events conducted by a religious organizations. *See, e.g., Rosenberger v. Rector and Visitors of the Univ. of Va.*, 515 U.S. 819, 843-44 (1995) (university should avoid distinguishing between evangelism, on the one hand, and the expression of ideas merely approved by a given religion); *Bob Jones Univ. v. United States*, 461 U.S. 574, 604 n.30 (1983) (avoiding potentially entangling inquiry into religious practice); *Widmar v. Vincent*, 454 U.S. 263, 269-70 n.6, 272 n.11 (1981) (holding that inquiries into the religious significance of words or events are to be avoided); *Thomas v. Review Bd.*, 450 U.S. 707, 715-16 (1981) (not within judicial function or competence to resolve religious differences); *Gillette v. United States*, 401 U.S. 437, 450 (1971) (Congress permitted to accommodate "all war" pacifists but not "just war" inductees because to broaden the exemption invites increased church-state entanglements and would render almost impossible the fair and uniform administration of selective service system); *Walz v. Tax Comm'n*, 397 U.S. 664, 674 (1970) (extolling the avoidance of entanglement that would otherwise follow if authorities made tax exemption contingent on social worth of religious social welfare programs); *cf. Mitchell v. Helms*, 530 U.S. 793, 828 (2000) (referring with approval to this line of precedent as a rationale for abandoning the "pervasively sectarian" test).

[18] *See* Carl H. Esbeck, *The Establishment Clause as a Structural Restraint on Governmental Power*, 1 Iowa Law Review 1-113 (1998).

[19] To have failed to have broadened 702 also would have led to serious entanglement of another kind, namely to lawsuits by employees outside the organization's faith community alleging claims of hostile work environment or religious harassment. *See* Michael Wolf, et al., *Religion in the Workplace: A Comprehensive Guide To Legal Rights and Responsibilities* 55-66, 157-62 (1998).

freedom of religious staffing for religious educational institutions,[20] and also allows for the accommodation of religion as a "bona fide occupational qualification."[21]

1. The Constitutionality of the Section 702(a) Freedom

In the mid-1980s a court challenge raised the claim that 702(a) was an unconstitutional "preference" for religious employers over secular employers. Without a single dissenting vote, the U.S. Supreme Court in *Corporation of the Presiding Bishop v. Amos*[22] upheld the 1972 amendment that broadened 702(a).[23] What Congress did by enlarging the scope of 702(a) was to lift a regulatory burden from religion. It did so even though the burden was imposed on secular employers similarly situated. That is not unconstitutional, held the Court, because the government does not "make [a] law respecting an establishment of religion"[24] by leaving religious groups alone. As the Supreme Court observed in *Amos*:

---

[20] *See* § 703(e)(2) of Title VII, 42 U.S.C. § 2000e-2(e)(2). This section is likely redundant to 702(a), which covers all religious employers including educational institutions. Thus, 703(e)(2) is not separately discussed in this monograph.

[21] Title VII provides that "it shall not be an unlawful employment practice" for any employer to "hire and employ employees" on the basis of "religion, sex, or national origin . . . where religion, sex, or national origin is a bona fide occupational qualification reasonably necessary to the normal operation of that particular business or enterprise." 42 U.S.C. § 2000e-2(e)(1). When it comes to religion, the provision has not been widely applied. While the provision's scope as to religion is thus undeveloped, it can be said that as a general matter the BFOQ exemption is read narrowly. A BFOQ may permit an employer, religious or secular, to discriminate in hiring based on religion, but only if the religious condition is essential to the performance of the job and affects the central duties of the job. Business necessity, not convenience or preference, must be proven by the employer. Michael Wolf, et al., *Religion in the Workplace: A Comprehensive Guide to Legal Rights and Responsibilities* 23-26 (1998).

[22] 483 U.S. 327 (1987).

[23] *Id.* Justice White wrote the majority opinion. Justice Brennan wrote an opinion concurring in the judgment, joined by Justice Marshall. *Id.* at 340. Justice Blackmun wrote an opinion concurring in the judgment, joined by Justice O'Connor. *Id.* at 346.

[24] The First Amendment provides, in relevant part, as follows: "Congress shall make no law respecting an establishment of religion, or prohibiting the free exercise thereof . . . ." U.S. CONST. AMEND. I.

> A law is not unconstitutional simply because it *allows* churches to advance religion, which is their very purpose. For a law to have [a] forbidden "effect" under [the Establishment Clause], it must be fair to say that the *government itself* has advanced religion through its own activities and influence.[25]

Similarly, the Court said that 702(a) was not a violation of equal protection because the hiring freedom it acknowledges is "rationally related to the legitimate purpose of alleviating significant governmental interference with the ability of religious organizations to define and carry out their religious missions."[26]

To have failed to broaden the scope of 702 risked a challenge that the original exemption invited unconstitutional entanglement between church and state. An appellate court in Maryland has since handed down a ruling much to that effect. The Maryland court sustained a constitutional challenge by a church-affiliated K-12 school to a limited exemption in a county employment nondiscrimination ordinance. The religious school had been sued under the ordinance when it dismissed two teachers because they were not members of the sponsoring church. The ordinance's exemption for religious staffing by a religious organization, which was only for jobs with "purely religious functions," was found unconstitutionally narrow. The court reasoned that the administration of the overly narrow exemption invited governmental interference with the internal management of religious organizations. The ordinance would require the court to define what was "purely religious" and what was "secular enough."[27] Such entanglement

---

[25] 483 U.S. at 337. This was not a new development. The Supreme Court had previously sustained religion-specific exemptions from regulatory burdens in the face of challenges under the Establishment Clause. *See Gillette v. United States*, 401 U.S. 437 (1971) (holding religious exemption from military draft for those who oppose all war does not violate Establishment Clause); *Zorach v. Clauson*, 343 U.S. 306 (1952) (finding release-time program for students to attend religious exercises off public school grounds does not violate Establishment Clause); *Arver v. United States*, 245 U.S. 366 (1918) (holding military draft service exemptions for clergy and theology students does not violate Establishment Clause).

[26] *Amos*, 483 U.S. at 339.

[27] *Montrose Christian School Corp. v. Walsh*, 770 A.2d 111, 124 (Md. App. 2001). The Supreme Court's church autonomy doctrine was relied upon, a line of cases that has its origin in the institutional

was seen to violate the church's First Amendment autonomy.

Similarly, the Federal Communications Commission (FCC) in the past required radio stations owned by religious organizations not to discriminate in employment on the basis of religion. There was a limited exemption but it was only for those jobs with duties that had a substantial connection to the content of the religious programming at a religious station. Realizing that enforcement of the regulation with the overly narrow exemption interfered with the religious autonomy of religious radio stations, in late 1998 the FCC announced that it would henceforth permit religious staffing in all employment positions at religious broadcasters.[28]

As these cases indicate, the staffing freedom acknowledged by 702(a) not only does not constitute a "preference" in violation of the Establishment Clause but the expanded section is likely required by the First Amendment to keep government from unconstitutionally entangling itself with faith-based organizations.

2. The Relevance of Religious Staffing to the Provision of Social Services

Unable to challenge directly the constitutionality of the broad scope of the religious staffing freedom acknowledged in 702(a), opponents of the faith-based initiative have tried to belittle its necessity. "What difference can it make to a Catholic soup kitchen," they ask, "if a Baptist is hired to ladle the soup?" Similarly, "Why should it matter to a Lutheran homeless shelter if a Jewish person is in charge of providing clean beds to people off the streets?" This line of argumentation is reductionist, of course, paring down a faith-driven ministry to the mere supply of bread and beds.

---

separation of church and state. *Id.* at 123-24.

[28]The FCC's proposed rules revising the equal employment regulations for broadcasters appear at 63 Fed. Reg. 66104 (Dec. 1, 1998). The final regulation provides: "Religious radio broadcasters may establish religious belief or affiliation as a job qualification for all station employees." 47 C.F.R. § 73.2080(a).

31

We have the proper response to this criticism from Justice William Brennan. In *Corporation of the Presiding Bishop v. Amos*, as we have seen, the Supreme Court unanimously held that a determination of the relevance or irrelevance of religion to particular staff positions within a faith-based organization must to be left to the sole judgment of each organization, lest the government excessively interfere with religion. Writing separately in *Amos*, Justice Brennan made an additional point, one properly recognizing the spiritual promptings that motivate people of faith to pursue their vocation in a religiously driven ministry:

> For many individuals, religious activity derives meaning in large measure from participation in a larger religious community. Such a community represents an ongoing tradition of shared beliefs, an organic entity not reducible to a mere aggregation of individuals. Determining that certain activities are in furtherance of an organization's religious mission, and that only those committed to that mission should conduct them, is thus a means by which a religious community defines itself. Solicitude for a church's ability to do so reflects the idea that furtherance of the autonomy of religious organizations often furthers individual religious freedom as well.

> . . . [W]e deem it vital that, if certain activities constitute part of a religious community's practice, then a religious organization should be able to require that only members of its community perform those activities.[29]

Of course, not every faith-based organization considers it crucial that all of its employees be of compatible faith. Some require only executive staff to be of a particular faith, or insist only that employees not openly contradict the beliefs of the organization. Some deliberately hire people of a variety of faiths or include employees without regard to religious belief. And while some faith-based organizations deliberately cultivate a religious environment, others for religious reasons just as deliberately avoid the overt appearance of religiosity. As the California Supreme Court recently

---

[29]*Amos*, 483 U.S. at 342-43.

observed of a Catholic hospital that fired an employee for "soul saving" on the job, "maintaining a secular appearance in its medical facility that is welcoming to all faiths, thereby de-emphasizing its distinctively Catholic affiliation, appears to be part of [the hospital's] religiously inspired mission of offering health care to the community."[30] All of these faith-based approaches to ministry, and their corresponding employment practices, are protected under the religious staffing freedom that Congress has acknowledged in 702(a).[31]

B. Religious Staffing Where Federal Funds Are Involved

Opponents of religious staffing concede, as they must after *Corporation of the Presiding Bishop v. Amos*, the facial constitutionality of the broad

---

[30]*Silo v. CHW Medical Foundation*, 45 P.3d 1162, 1170 (Cal. 2002) (dismissing Protestant employee's claim of religious discrimination because Catholic hospital had First Amendment autonomy to exercise control over the religious speech of its employees).

[31]The general religious staffing freedom in 702(a) should be distinguished from the so-called "ministerial exception" to Title VII. The ministerial exception is a right derived by the courts from the First Amendment. Michael Wolf, et al., *Religion in the Workplace: A Comprehensive Guide to Legal Rights and Responsibilities* 12-13 (1998). Employment decisions concerning clergy and other religious ministers, when acting within the scope of their duties as ministers, are deemed exempt from all employment discrimination claims. This includes not just claims of religious discrimination, but also discrimination motivated by race, sex, national origin, and the like. *See, e.g., Rayburn v. General Conf. of Seventh-day Adventists*, 772 F.2d 1165 (4th Cir. 1985) (holding that for First Amendment reasons court could not consider sex discrimination claim by assistant minister against her church); *EEOC v. Southwestern Baptist Theological Seminary*, 651 F.2d 277 (5th Cir. 1981) (holding that seminary need not submit employment reports on its faculty to the EEOC because they are "ministers"); *McClure v. Salvation Army*, 460 F.2d 553 (5th Cir. 1972) (holding that for First Amendment reasons Title VII does not regulate the employment relationship between church and its minister). For more recent cases, *see Alicea-Hernandez v. Catholic Bishop of Chicago*, 320 F.3d 698 (7th Cir. 2003); *Bryce v. Episcopal Church in the Diocese of Colorado*, 289 F.3d 648 (10th Cir. 2002); *EEOC v. Roman Catholic Diocese of Raleigh*, 213 F.3d 795 (4th Cir. 2000); *Gellington v. Christian Methodist Episcopal Church, Inc.*, 203 F.3d 1299 (11th Cir. 2000); *EEOC v. Catholic Univ. of Am.*, 83 F.3d 455 (D.C. Cir. 1996); *Young v. N. Ill. Conf. of United Methodist Church*, 21 F.3d 184 (7th Cir. 1994); *Natal v. Christian & Missionary Alliance*, 878 F.2d 1575 (1st Cir. 1989); *Hutchison v. Thomas*, 789 F.2d 392 (6th Cir. 1986). A faith-based organization's employees working in a directly funded social service program would generally not have resort to the ministerial exception. This is because the job tasks would not fit the job description of clergy or minister. (A special case might be presented where an employee had mixed duties, partly ministerial and partly the delivery of government-funded social services.) From the viewpoint of the government, a religious provider's staff is performing secular work, that is, the delivery of social services. That is so, albeit from the viewpoint of the provider and its staff they are religiously motivated in their vocation of helping the poor.

scope of 702(a). But, they argue, if a faith-based organization receives federal funds then things are different, and various consequences flow from that difference. Each of their arguments is mistaken.

1. Is 702(a) Forfeited When a Faith-Based Organization Receives Government Funds?

Opponents begin by arguing that the broad hiring freedom in 702(a) is forfeited when a faith-based organization accepts a government grant or other financial assistance.[32] However, every court to rule on this claim has rejected it.[33] The rationale of the courts is quite interesting.

As noted previously, 702(a) acknowledges that religious organizations are not subject to Title VII's prohibition on employment discrimination when it comes to their making employment decisions on the grounds of religion. Section 702(a) begins "This title shall not apply, . . ." indicating, say the courts, a congressional decision that the scope of Title VII does not

---

[32]By a simple comparison of Title VI with Title VII of the Civil Rights Act of 1964, it is apparent that the opponents' argument makes little sense. When Congress intended to trigger nondiscrimination duties based on the receipt of federal financial assistance Congress so provided in Title VI—not Title VII. Title VI prohibits discrimination by recipients of federal aid. The prohibited bases of discrimination are race, color, and national origin. 42 U.S.C. § 2000d et al. But Congress did not see fit to provide for religion as a prohibited basis of discrimination when federal grants and other assistance are involved. Obviously that was quite intentional by Congress.

[33]See Hall v. Baptist Memorial Health Care Corp., 215 F.3d 618, 625 (6ᵗʰ Cir. 2000) (dismissing religious discrimination claim filed by employee against religious organization because organization was not subject to Title VII and the receipt of substantial government funding did not bring about a waiver of the exemption); Siegel v. Truett-McConnell College, 13 F. Supp.2d 1335, 1343-45 (N.D. Ga. 1994), aff'd, 73 F.3d 1108 (11ᵗʰ Cir. 1995) (table) (dismissing religious discrimination claim filed by faculty member against religious college because college was not subject to Title VII and the receipt of substantial government funding did not bring about a waiver of 702(a)); Young v. Shawnee Mission Medical Center, 1988 U.S. Dist. LEXIS 12248 (D. Kan. Oct 21, 1988) (holding that religious hospital did not lose the benefit of 702(a) merely because it received federal Medicare payments; see also Egan v. Hamline United Methodist Church, 679 N.W.2d 350, 356-58 (Minn. App. 2004) (holding that religious exemption in state human rights act is not waived by statements of a church); Arriaga v. Loma Linda University, 13 Cal. Rptr.2d 619 (Cal. App. 1992) (holding that religious exemption in state employment nondiscrimination law was not lost merely because religious college received state funding). In addition, a legal opinion by the Office of Legal Counsel at the U.S. Department of Justice concluded that 702(a) is not forfeited when a religious organization receives federal funding. Memorandum for Brett Kavanaugh, Associate White House Counsel, from Sheldon Bradshaw, Deputy Assistant Attorney General, Office of Legal Counsel, U.S. Department of Justice (June 25, 2001).

even encompass, in the first instance, a religious organization's religious staffing practices.[34] In this interpretation, then, 702(a) is not a mere statutory privilege that can, upon particular conduct of the employer, be lost or waived.[35] Rather, Title VII in its scope simply does not reach the conduct of religious staffing by religious organizations. No action by a religious organization—for example, its acceptance of a government grant—can change this congressionally limited scope of Title VII.

The courts did not stop there, however. There was a reason Congress circumscribed the scope of Title VII in this manner. It was because to do otherwise risked violating the First Amendment autonomy of religious employers.[36] As stated by one circuit court, "The exemptions reflect a decision by Congress that religious organizations have a constitutional right to be free from government intervention."[37] Normally a statutory provision like 702(a) is a carve-out, if you will, relieving an individual or organization from an otherwise applicable regulatory obligation. Section 702(a) is not an exemption or "privilege" in that sense, say these appellate courts, but an acknowledgement by Congress of the First Amendment autonomy of religious organizations.

2. Doesn't Acceptance of Government Funds Turn Faith-Based Providers into "Public" Social-Service Agencies?

Opponents of religious staffing freedom next argue that if a

---

[34]*Little v. Wuerl*, 929 F.2d 944, 951 (3d Cir. 1991); *Hall v. Baptist Memorial Health Care Corp.*, 215 F.3d 618, 625 (6th Cir. 2000).

[35]*Little*, 929 F.2d at 951; *Siegel*, 13 F. Supp.2d at 1345. As a matter of simple logic this interpretation of 702(a) equally applies to a situation where a faith-based organization, having just received a grant, makes new hires so as to fulfill the terms of the grant.

[36]*Little*, 929 F.2d at 946-51; *Hall*, 215 F.3d at 625; *Egan*, 679 N.W.2d at 357-58.

[37]*Hall*, 215 F.3d at 625. *Accord Egan*, 679 N.W.2d at 358 ("We conclude that the constitutional policy of avoiding entanglement controls in this case.").

government-funded faith-based provider can invoke 702(a), then 702(a) must violate the Establishment Clause. This makes no sense. Section 702(a) keeps government out of the internal business of a religious organization's governance rather than mixing the two. That honors the Establishment Clause rather than violating it. This is why the section was expanded by Congress in 1972—to "take the political hands of Caesar off the institutions of God, where they have no place to be," as Senator Sam Ervin said.

The opponents of the faith-based initiative suppose that there is a direct nexus between the government's social-service programs and the religious staffing decisions of a faith-based provider. This is not the case. The purpose of the government programs is not to boost the hiring of unemployed social workers. That would be a jobs program. Rather, the object of the government's programs is the provision of social services to the poor and needy. Whether a service provider that receives government monies also happens to hire people on a religious basis is unlikely even to be known to the government. But whether known or not, it is the faith-based provider, of course, that is making the staffing decisions, not the government. Such a private decision cannot violate the Establishment Clause of the First Amendment. The Bill of Rights, including the Establishment Clause, was adopted to restrain only government, not the independent sector. The Establishment Clause cannot be violated if the government has not even made the employment decision being questioned.[38]

---

[38] The lack of "federal action" or "state action" here is analogous to the Supreme Court's rationale for sustaining the constitutionality of "indirect" funding cases such as those involving school vouchers. *See Zelman v. Simmons-Harris*, 536 U.S. 639 (2002) (upholding state K-12 school voucher program open to a broad class of schools, including religious schools). When the parents of a school-age child, empowered with an educational voucher, make an independent choice of where to enroll their child, the Establishment Clause is not implicated when the aid goes to a religious school as a result of the private choice. Like the choice of these parents, the private choice by a faith-based organization concerning religious staffing does not implicate the government/grantor as the "causal actor." Hence the staffing decision does not incur Establishment Clause scrutiny. This is just another way of demonstrating that the opposition's argument here proves too much, for if faith-based organizations are "federal actors" for the purposes of their employment, they are "federal actors" for all other things that they do. Yet there is wide agreement that such a result is absurd. The mere receipt of a government grant cannot be the legal equivalent of "nationalizing" an independent-sector charity.

Because there is no nexus between the government's awarding of the grant funding and the employment practices, a faith-based organization's religious staffing is neither "state action" under the Fourteenth Amendment nor "federal action" under the Fifth Amendment. In *Rendell-Baker v. Kohn*,[39] a teacher sued a private school alleging denial of her constitutional rights as an employee. The U.S. Supreme Court dismissed. The Court reasoned that, just because the school received most of its funding from the state it did not thereby become a "state actor." Similarly, in *Blum v. Yaretsky*,[40] the Supreme Court held that the pervasive regulation of private nursing homes, along with the receipt of considerable government funding, did not render a nursing home's decision on patient level-of-care "state action."[41] The same principle holds for faith-based social-service providers.

Critics of the religious staffing freedom argue that 702(a) is different, for when Congress enacted the section it expressly authorized religious organizations to discriminate in employment on the basis of religion. Thus, these critics reason, the discrimination can be attributed to Congress as an intentional governmental act. The law, however, is to the contrary. In *Flagg Brothers, Inc. v. Brooks*,[42] for example, the U.S. Supreme Court rejected a constitutional challenge by a debtor to a statute in a state's commercial code where the legislature expressly allowed for self-help by a creditor in collecting certain debts. The Court found no "state action," notwithstanding the legislature's enactment of the statute, whereby the self-help acts of creditors were explicitly authorized to the detriment of debtors. The statute

---

[39] 457 U.S. 830 (1982).

[40] 457 U.S. 991 (1982).

[41] The Supreme Court's holdings in *Rendell-Baker* and *Blum* clearly overturned the result in an earlier, lower-court decision involving a private, secular social-service provider. *See Robinson v. Price*, 553 F.2d 918 (5th Cir. 1977) (reversing dismissal on the pleadings and remanding for factual inquiry into whether a private, secular social-service provider was a "state actor" because, *inter alia*, it received government grant monies). *Robinson* is also distinguishable because eight members of the provider's board of directors were appointed by local government and all funding requests had first to be approved by local officials. Those facts, alleged the plaintiff, arguably made the provider a joint public/private program. Such heightened government involvement does not occur with the faith-based initiative.

[42] 436 U.S. 149, 164 (1978). *Accord American Mfrs. Mut. Ins. Co. v. Sullivan*, 526 U.S. 40, 54 (1999).

was permissive rather than mandatory, reasoned the Court, and thus the actions of creditors utilizing self-help were not attributable to the state. Section 702(a) is likewise permissive. It allows religious staffing but it does not require it.[43]

The U.S. Supreme Court has also examined the operation of 702(a) and the religious staffing question and observed that religious discrimination does not constitute "federal action" attributable to the federal government. In the passage from *Corporation of the Presiding Bishop v. Amos* quoted above, the Court held that 702(a) simply "allows" religious groups to advance religion; hence, it is not fair to say that the "government itself" is responsible for the religious staffing.[44] Moreover, the employee in *Amos*, who had lost his job for falling into spiritual disfavor with his church, argued that the failure of Title VII to protect him from religious discrimination denied him rights under the Free Exercise Clause. The Court, however, said it need not reach that free exercise claim because the threshold question of whether there was "federal action" must be answered in the negative:

---

[43]Opponents of the faith-based initiative also cite *Norwood v. Harrison*, 413 U.S. 455 (1973). *Norwood* is not applicable. The case came at a time when Southerners were opening private, segregated academies to avoid public school desegregation. Eradication of racially segregated public schools is a constitutional duty of the state. In response, the Court was aggressive in piercing through paper veils that purported to erect public/private distinctions. The Court's aim was, of course, to reverse the larger pattern of racially segregated schools. In that vein, *Norwood* held unconstitutional a program for loaning textbooks to private K-12 schools, including religious schools, because the program undermined the duty to desegregate public schools.

The circumstances before us concerning the faith-based initiative are quite different. To permit faith-based organizations to staff on a religious basis undercuts no duty of the state to ensure that it refrain from religious discrimination. Indeed, the aim of the faith-based initiative is to protect the free exercise of religion by stopping past religious discrimination against the funding of many religious organizations. To demonstrate that aid to racially discriminatory schools is quite different than protecting free exercise, the *Norwood* Court stressed that "the Constitution . . . places no value on discrimination as it does on the values inherent in the Free Exercise Clause." *Id.* at 469-70.

To read *Norwood* as applicable here is not only contrary to the Court's own limitations on Norwood, but it would put *Norwood* at odds with *Amos, Rendell-Baker, Blum,* and *Flagg Brothers,* all more recent decisions. That would call into question whether *Norwood* even survives. *Norwood* remains good law, but it is confined to its terms and its times.

[44]*Amos*, 483 U.S. at 337 (1987).

Undoubtedly, [the employee]'s freedom of choice in religious matters was impinged upon, but it was the Church . . . and not the Government, who put him to the choice of changing his religious practices or losing his job.[45]

Just as the *Amos* Court held that without "federal action" by the government there can be no Free Exercise Clause violation as a result of 702(a), likewise without "federal action" by the government there can be no Establishment Clause violation.

3. Isn't the Religious Staffing Freedom a Religious "Preference" in Violation of the Establishment Clause?

We have seen that the lack of "federal action" is an insurmountable hurdle to any claim that the Establishment Clause is violated. However, even if opponents to the faith-based initiative were to get a court to address the merits of their Establishment Clause argument, they would fail.

The opponents begin by attempting to characterize 702(a) as religious favoritism or a "preference."[46] How is it, they ask, that all other providers comply without complaint with the nondiscrimination regulations, whereas religious providers get to carry a lighter regulatory load because of 702(a)? But this criticism misapprehends the principle of substantive neutrality in church-state relations. Neutrality is where the government acknowledges that the freedom to staff on a religious basis secures for faith-based organizations the same freedom that other mission-driven organizations already have. The Sierra Club may hire only those who are committed to the environmental movement. The Libertarian Party may prefer those who are devoted to market solutions. And Planned Parenthood may screen for

---

[45]*Id.* at 337 n.15.

[46]*See Egan v. Hamline United Methodist Church*, 697 N.W.2d 350, 357-59 (Minn. App. 2004), where a state provision similar to 702(a) was attacked as a "preference" in violation of the Establishment Clause. The court held that not only did the exemption not violate the Establishment Clause but it served one of the underlying purposes of the clause, which is non-entanglement between church and state.

those prospective employees who are pro-choice. While a restriction on religious hiring does not constrain Sierra Club, the Libertarian Party, or Planned Parenthood, for religion is irrelevant to their missions, such a restriction does restrain the faith-based provider. As a matter of true neutrality, then, faith-based organizations must be able to employ those of like-minded faith.[47]

It follows that religious staffing is not a "preference" in violation of the Establishment Clause. Indeed, this principle of substantive neutrality reinforces the separation of church and state. As law professor Douglas Laycock has said in congressional testimony:

> To say that a religious provider must conceal or suppress its religious identity . . . or hire people who are not committed to its mission . . . uses the government's power of the purse to coerce people to abandon religious practices . . . . Charitable choice provisions that protect the religious liberty of religious providers are pro-separation; they separate the religious choices of commitments of the American people from government influence.[48]

A substantively neutral policy concerning funding for social services is one that enables both secular and faith-based providers an opportunity to compete for grants without being forced to deny their essential character as either secular or religious. Secular providers can and should be able to choose staff committed to the organization's secular mission, be it environmentalism, libertarianism, or reproductive rights. For them, religion

---

[47]"Imagine the reaction of the World Wildlife Fund—which has received more than $115 million in Federal support since 1996—if it were required to hire employees without regard to their position on environmental conservation. Or that of Planned Parenthood—the recipient of millions of Federal dollars each year—if it had to hire staff without considering their views on abortion or birth control. Some people agree with the missions of these organizations, others do not. But no one can deny that these organizations' ability to execute their goals hinges on whether they may choose to hire like-minded people." White House Office of Faith-Based and Community Initiatives, *Protecting the Civil Rights and Religious Liberty of Faith-Based Organizations: Why Religious Hiring Rights Must be Preserved* 3 (2003), *available at* <http://www. whitehouse.gov/government/fbci/booklet.pdf>. *Reprinted in* Appendix 8.

[48]*The Constitutional Role of Faith-Based Organizations in Competitions for Federal Social Service Funds*, Testimony by Douglas Laycock; before the House Subcomm. on the Constitution, Comm. On the Judiciary, 107th Cong., 23 (June 7, 2001) *available at* <http://www.house.gov/judiciary/72981.pdf>.

is an irrelevant criterion. In the same way, faith-based organizations, for whom religion is the defining characteristic, must be able to select staff who are committed to the provider's faith-defined vision. Moreover, a substantively neutral social-service program is one that does not skew the choices of beneficiaries toward or away from religious social-service providers. If the poor and needy are to have both secular and religious choices, then 702(a) is needed to attract the participation of religious charities and to safeguard their religious character from overly invasive regulation.

Opponents of the faith-based initiative persist in their argument that their case is different. They insist that the situation is not simply that faith-based organizations receive federal assistance to deliver services and that they happen, unrelatedly, to discriminate in employment. Rather, say these opponents, religious charities receive program monies and then are discriminating in those very programs. But this is a distinction without a difference. The fact remains that the government makes its competitive grant awards on a basis that is wholly independent of a religious provider's decision to staff on a religious basis. As the Court pointed out in the *Amos* decision, it is not unconstitutional for government to allow religious charities to pursue their own interests, which is their very purpose.[49] For government to violate the Establishment Clause it must be possible to say that the government itself has advanced religion. All the government has set out to do is to help the poor and needy by awarding its grant monies to the most effective and efficient applicants. If faith-based organizations win some of these awards and deliver the services to the poor, all while obeying First Amendment guidelines on direct government funding, then that is the end of the constitutional oversight.[50]

---

[49]*Amos*, 483 U.S. at 337 (1987).

[50]*Cf. Columbia Union College v. Oliver*, 254 F.3d 496 (4th Cir. 2001), where the court upheld a state program providing general aid to colleges, including religiously affiliated colleges. The funding was not unconstitutional, as applied to a Seventh-day Adventist college, notwithstanding that the college "gave an express preference in hiring . . . to members of the Church." *Id.* at 508.

A state appeals court followed just such Establishment Clause logic in a faith-based employment case, albeit one not involving 702(a). In *Saucier v. Employment Security Department,*[51] a state agency and a faith-based drug rehabilitation center were sued by a former counselor employed at the religious center. The plaintiff had been laid off and now sought unemployment compensation payments. The drug rehabilitation center, as a religious organization, was exempt under state law from paying unemployment compensation taxes. Hence, unemployment benefits were unavailable to the plaintiff. The rehabilitation center was a recipient of federal and state grants. When unemployment benefits were denied to the plaintiff, she argued that the government grants, when juxtaposed with the religious rehabilitation center's tax exemption, violated the Establishment Clause. The plaintiff's argument in *Saucier* parallels the opponents' claim that a federal social-service grant, when juxtaposed with 702(a), violates the Establishment Clause. The court in *Saucier* found that there was no nexus between the tax exemption and the faith-based organization's receipt of government monies.[52] Hence, the plaintiff's claim was dismissed as without merit.

The rationale of the court in *Saucier* is equally applicable to those who oppose religious staffing by faith-based organizations. There is no constitutionally salient nexus between the award of a government social-service grant and the staffing freedom reflected in 702(a).

---

[51] 954 P.2d 285 (Wash. App. 1998).

[52] *Id.* at 288-89. The court of appeals noted that the exemption for faith-based organizations from state unemployment taxes had been litigated elsewhere and found not to violate the Establishment Clause. The court relied on *Rojas v. Fitch*, 127 F.3d 184 (1st Cir. 1997).

4. Doesn't the *Dodge* Case Prove that Religious Staffing is Illegal for Government-Funded Faith-Based Providers?

Opponents of religious staffing can point to only one case to buttress their argument, but reliance on that shaky precedent merely evidences the level of desperation in their position. The case is *Dodge v. Salvation Army*,[53] an unpublished opinion in a lawsuit filed in a federal trial court in Mississippi.

In *Dodge*, the local Salvation Army had received over time various federal and state funds to operate a domestic violence shelter. The Salvation Army used a recently awarded federal grant to upgrade an existing employee, Ms. Jamie Dodge, from part-time to full-time status in the position of Victims' Assistance Coordinator. Although the grant was not a jobs program, Salvation Army had discretion to use the monies as it did, namely to upgrade Ms. Dodge's employment status. When Ms. Dodge was first hired she had indicated she was Catholic. Soon after her job was made full time Ms. Dodge was discovered using the office photocopy machine for unauthorized personal use, copying "manuals and information on Satanic/Wiccan rituals." The Salvation Army dismissed Ms. Dodge, citing both her unauthorized use of office materials and her "occult practices that are inconsistent with the religious purposes of the Salvation Army."

Ms. Dodge quickly brought suit under Title VII of the 1964 Civil Rights Act, alleging employment discrimination on the basis of religion. The Salvation Army, in turn, raised 702(a) in its defense. The Mississippi court ruled that 702(a), if applied to the facts in this case, would violate the Establishment Clause.

The court's ruling against the Salvation Army's reliance on 702(a) is a

---

[53]1989 WL 53857 (S.D. Miss. 1989).

model of muddled logic. In part that may have been because the federal agency that had awarded the grant to the Salvation Army was not made a party to Ms. Dodge's lawsuit. Hence, the federal government's lawyers were not present before the court to be heard on the matter and to urge a proper interpretation of the Establishment Clause. Additionally, given that only government can violate the Establishment Clause and that the federal agency awarding the grant was not brought into the lawsuit as a defendant, the court should never have entertained Ms. Dodge's argument that the clause was violated. The judge's eventual holding that 702(a) was unconstitutional, as applied to Ms. Dodge's job, was of doubtful rationale when handed down in 1989 and, given subsequent developments, is clearly not the law today.[54]

The *Dodge* court declined to follow the Supreme Court decision most directly on point, namely *Corporation of the Presiding Bishop v. Amos*, which just two years before had unanimously upheld the application of 702(a) in the case of a janitor with secular duties at a church-operated facility. Instead the trial court reasoned from a fifteen-year-old case that was essentially irrelevant, namely *Lemon v. Kurtzman*.[55] In *Lemon* the Supreme Court had held that the job of a teacher at a K-12 religious school so integrates religious and secular functions that the government cannot, consistent with the Establishment Clause, fund even part of a parochial school teacher's salary. The *Dodge* case, however, involved a job with essentially secular functions (janitor) and thus a job clearly eligible for government funding. Thus *Amos*—not *Lemon*—unquestionably applied to Ms. Dodge's job at the Salvation Army. This was not a close case, and thus there was absolutely no need even to consider *Lemon* and a possible violation of the Establishment Clause.

---

[54]The criticism of the *Dodge* case that appears in the text to follow was taken in substantial part from a July, 2001, letter from Douglas Laycock, Professor of Law at the University of Texas – Austin, to Senator Patrick Leahy, Chair of the Senate Judiciary Committee.

[55]403 U.S. 602 (1971).

We do not mean to suggest that 702(a) requires, or even allows, a distinction between secular and religious jobs. The 1972 amendment rejected any such distinction. We only mean to show that, even under the older secular/religious distinction that the Supreme Court insisted on back in the days of *Lemon*, the situation in *Dodge* was an easy case because the job in question was essentially secular. This makes the trial court's logic in *Dodge* even more befuddling.[56]

More important, since *Dodge* was handed down the Supreme Court has all but abandoned the strict no-aid-to-religion reasoning that undergirded the analysis in the *Lemon* case and thus the *Dodge* decision.[57] This broad trend in the Supreme Court in favor of the rule of neutrality in government aid programs wholly undercuts the *Dodge* court's overly suspicious reaction to government funding of religious social-service providers.

Contrary to the result in *Dodge*, the constitutionality of 702(a) when a faith-based provider receives government funds more nearly parallels a dispute that arose over whether Congress could, without running afoul of the Establishment Clause, provide religious hospitals with funding under the Hill-Burton Act.[58] The act provides federal funding for capital improvements at hospitals, whether public or private, secular or religious.

---

[56]Unfortunately *Dodge* was never tested on appeal. The Salvation Army settled the case before trial rather than incur more litigation expenses.

[57]Since the 1989 opinion in *Dodge*, five important cases have come down upholding the distribution of government benefits on a neutral basis to nongovernmental organizations, including the pervasively religious. *See Zelman v. Simmons-Harris*, 536 U.S. 639 (2002); *Mitchell v. Helms*, 530 U.S. 793 (2000); *Agostini v. Felton*, 521 U.S. 203 (1997); *Rosenberger v. Rector and Visitors of the Univ. of Va.*, 515 U.S. 819 (1995); *Zobrest v. Catalina Foothills School Dist.*, 509 U.S. 1 (1993). Four other important cases restricting the distribution of government aid to religious organizations, good law at the time of *Dodge*, have since been overruled in whole or substantial part. *See Wolman v. Walter*, 433 U.S. 229 (1977), *overruled in Mitchell v. Helms*, 530 U.S. 793, 835, 837 (2000); *Meek v. Pittenger*, 421 U.S. 349 (1975), *overruled in Mitchell v. Helms*, 530 U.S. 793, 835, 837 (2000); *Aguilar v. Felton*, 473 U.S. 402 (1985), *overruled in Agostini v. Felton*, 521 U.S. 203, 235 (1997); *School Dist. of Grand Rapids v. Ball*, 473 U.S. 373 (1985), *overruled in part in Agostini v. Felton*, 521 U.S. 203, 235 (1997).

[58]The full title of the Hill-Burton Act is the Hospital Survey and Construction Act of 1946, 42 U.S.C. §§ 291-291o-1.

Some of the funded religious hospitals refused to provide abortions and sterilizations because of religious doctrine. Patients seeking those reproductive services complained that for the federal government to fund these hospitals constituted the promotion of religious belief contrary to the Establishment Clause.

Congress disagreed, however, and sought to codify its view of the matter into the act by adopting an amendment offered by Democratic Senator Frank Church (Idaho). The so-called "Church Amendment" provided that the receipt of any grant under the Hill-Burton Act by a hospital did "not authorize any court or public official to require . . . [s]uch entity to . . . make its facilities available for the performance of any sterilization procedure or abortion if the performance of such procedure or abortion in such facilities is prohibited by the entity on the basis of religious beliefs or moral convictions." [59]

The Church Amendment was quickly challenged in the courts as a violation of the Establishment Clause, with the claimants juxtaposing the government's financial support under the Hill-Burton Act with the religious exemption codified by the Church Amendment. The federal courts held that Congress, far from seeking to establish religion, had only sought to preserve neutrality in the face of religious and moral differences.[60] As such, the courts had little trouble upholding the Church Amendment. A religious hospital's refusal to provide certain reproductive services is a wholly

---

[59] Section 401(b) of the Health Programs Extension Act of 1973, Pub. L. No. 93-45, 87 Stat. 91, 95 (codified at 42 U.S.C. § 300a-7).

[60] See Chrisman v. Sisters of St. Joseph of Peace, 506 F.2d 308, 311-12 (9th Cir. 1974) (holding that Church Amendment reflects the congressional view that Hill-Burton grantees are not acting under color of law); Taylor v. St. Vincent's Hospital, 523 F.2d 75, 77 (9th Cir. 1975) (same); cf. Seale v. Jasper Hospital Dist. and Jasper Memorial Hospital Foundation, Inc., 1997 WL 606857 *4-*5 (Tex. App. Oct. 2, 1997) (finding religious hospital does not waive its right to refuse to perform sterilizations and abortions merely because it had a lease with the government on its building). The cases further observe that religious hospitals have free exercise rights, and those rights cannot be forfeited as a condition of qualifying for federal funding. See Doe v. Bellin Memorial Hospital, 479 F.2d 756, 761 (7th Cir. 1973).

private act, not "federal action." The Church Amendment simply permitted religious hospitals to be true to their religious beliefs and practices. A legislature does not establish religion by leaving it alone.

Section 702(a) likewise places the government in a position of religious neutrality. The government's objective in making awards to independent-sector providers is to implement the most effective and efficient social-service program. Whether or not a grantee in the independent sector staffs on a religious basis has no nexus to the government's social-service goals; hence, the Establishment Clause is not implicated.

5. Don't Taxpayers Have a Right Not to Be Forced to Support Faith-Based Organizations They Consider Objectionable?

On occasion, opponents of the faith-based initiative attack religious social-service organizations that staff on a religious basis by claiming that federal taxpayers have a personal right of conscience not to have their taxes awarded to religious organizations. The purported legal claim is that taxpayers have a constitutional right not to be coerced into supporting a religion they do not share, or a right not to be "religiously offended" when federal tax revenues end up in the accounts of a faith-based provider. Such pleas are often laced with out-of-context quotes about "not one pence" from James Madison or "sinful and tyrannical" actions from Thomas Jefferson.

This is mere rhetorical posturing that has no basis in constitutional law. The U.S. Supreme Court repeatedly has refused to recognize a federal taxpayer claim alleging coercion or other personal religious harm. In *Tilton v. Richardson,*[61] plaintiffs claimed that the payment of federal taxes into general revenues, some amount of which was awarded to church-related colleges along with secular institutions of higher education, caused them to suffer coercion in violation of the Free Exercise Clause. The Court found no

---

[61]403 U.S. 672 (1971).

plausible claim of religious compulsion, and thereby held that a federal taxpayer's cause of action for coercion of religious conscience failed to state a claim under the Free Exercise Clause.[62]

In *Valley Forge Christian College v. Americans United*,[63] plaintiffs challenged as unconstitutional the transfer of government surplus property to a religious college. This time the plaintiffs took the alternative tack of claiming an Establishment Clause violation. The Supreme Court, however, rebuffed all asserted bases for justiciability because the plaintiffs lacked the requisite personal "injury in fact" to have standing to sue. One of the rejected claims was that the plaintiffs had a "spiritual stake" in not having their government give away property to a religious organization of which they were not a member, or to otherwise act in a manner contrary, in their view, to the values inherent in the no-establishment of religion. The High Court rejected this characterization of plaintiffs' "injury" and held that an individualized "spiritual stake" in having one's government comply with the Establishment Clause is not a constitutionally recognized harm.[64]

As U.S. citizens our federal taxes support all manner of policies and programs with which we deeply disagree. Our taxes pay for the acquisition of nuclear arms and the infliction of capital punishment, both policies challenged in a venerable history of conscientious objection. Taxes pay the salaries of public officials whose policies we despise and oppose at every opportunity. None of these complaints give rise to constitutionally cognizable "injuries" to us as federal taxpayers. If they did, there would be no end to the lawsuits attempting to undo congressional appropriations. There is no reason that a federal taxpayer alleging "coercion of conscience" or being "religiously offended" by the award of government funds to a

---

[62] *Id.* at 689. To the same effect is *Bd. of Ed. of Central Sch. Dist. 1 v. Allen*, 392 U.S. 236, 248-49 (1968) (rejecting taxpayer's free exercise claim based on tax monies assisting religious K-12 schools).

[63] 454 U.S. 464 (1982).

[64] *Id.* at 486 n.22.

faith-based provider should, on the merits of the claim, be treated any differently.[65]

6. Doesn't Religious Staffing Open the Floodgates to Employment Discrimination More Generally?

Critics sometimes oppose religious staffing by claiming that permitting religious groups to be selective in employment on this limited basis is tantamount to authorizing them to discriminate more generally. They call for a renewal of the nation's historic commitment against discrimination of all kinds, particularly when government support is involved. While the motivation of these critics may be laudable and the goal of ending invidious discrimination is without a doubt praiseworthy, their criticism is misplaced.

Religious staffing is a limited freedom from otherwise applicable federal employment civil rights duties. It does not authorize faith-based organizations, having received government grants or contracts, to engage in religious discrimination against those people who seek their services. Indeed, the explicit policy of the faith-based initiative—as reflected in the Charitable Choice rules[66] and in the recently issued Executive Order 13279[67]—forbids discrimination against beneficiaries on the basis of religion. Nor does the freedom of religious staffing exempt faith-based

---

[65]Taxpayers, to be sure, have been accorded specialized standing to bring claims under the Establishment Clause when challenging the use of spending power. *See Flast v. Cohen*, 392 U.S. 83 (1968). But that limited grant of standing to sue, a matter that goes only to justiciability and not the merits, stops far short of saying that a personal, individualized claim of taxpayer "coercion of religious conscience" is meritorious. As stated in the text, *Valley Forge* rejected such a claim. Taxpayers will continue to be afforded specialized standing to sue under *Flast*. But opponents of the faith-based initiative cannot continue to posture for rhetorical advantage by claiming they have a "personal right" not to have their taxes, once paid into general revenues, going to faith-based organizations in the form of neutrally awarded federal grants.

[66]42 U.S.C. § 604a(g). *Reprinted in* Appendix 3.

[67]Consider the following statement among the "equal protection" principles in Executive Order 13279, 67 Fed. Reg. 77141 (Dec. 16, 2002): faith-based organizations providing services funded by the federal government are not permitted "to discriminate against current or prospective program beneficiaries on the basis of religion, a religious belief, a refusal to hold a religious belief, or a refusal to actively participate in a religious practice." *Id.* at 77142. The Executive Order is reprinted in Appendix 6.

organizations from complying with prohibitions on employment discrimination on bases other than religion. As noted previously, religious organizations covered by Title VII may not discriminate in employment on the grounds of race, color, sex, or national origin. Moreover, while other general federal nondiscrimination statutes also exempt religious hiring, they do not exempt religious organizations from the bans on discrimination on the basis of age or disability.

In certain instances the courts have held that 702(a) permits faith-based organizations to make employment decisions on the basis of sex or lifestyle. However, that is the case whether or not the religious organization has been awarded a federal social-service grant. Accordingly, the faith-based initiative does not alter the status quo when it comes to unlawful employment discrimination on the basis of sex or lifestyle.

a. Pregnancy and Discrimination on the Basis of Sex or Religion

Religious organizations with 15 or more employees are bound by Title VII's prohibition of discrimination on the basis of sex, including discrimination against a woman because of her pregnancy.[68] What, then, of a faith-based organization that dismisses a female employee because she is unmarried and pregnant, giving as its reason its sincerely held religious belief concerning sexual abstinence except within the bond of marriage? Is this a lawful religious staffing decision under 702(a), or actionable sex discrimination?

The federal courts, quite sensibly, have handled this situation as a question of fact. If the underlying motive for the discharge was religious, then the faith-based organization is absolved of the charge of discriminatory behavior.[69] However, to reach that decision, the religious organization's policy or practice toward its unmarried male employees is subject to

---

[68] 42 U.S.C. § 2000e(k).

[69] *See, e.g., Boyd v. Harding Academy of Memphis, Inc.,* 88 F.3d 410, 414 (6th Cir. 1996) (upholding the

examination. If the evidence shows that the rule of sexual abstinence is applied only to unmarried women—and not to promiscuous single males—then the courts understandably infer that the employer's real motive was based on sex rather than religion,[70] and the discharge is unlawful under Title VII. The rule of law is the same for faith-based organizations that receive federal funding for the provision of social-services. In other words, the faith-based initiative does not alter in any way the handling of these Title VII claims.

b. Homosexuality and Discrimination on the Basis of Religion

Title VII does not prohibit discrimination in employment on the basis of sexual orientation or homosexuality. This is true for all employers, secular and religious. And that does not change whether or not the employer receives federal financial assistance. However, what if the discrimination on the basis of sexual orientation is motivated by the employer's religious belief? Is that possibly actionable under Title VII as religious discrimination? The courts have answered in the negative, as explained below.

Title VII does prohibit secular employers from using an individual's religion as a criterion for hiring, promotion, or discharge, as well as preclude the use of an individual's failure to embrace the employer's religion or to join the employer's church as a job criterion. However, even a secular employer may prohibit employees from adopting certain lifestyles or behaviors—for example, homosexual practice—without necessarily engaging in religious discrimination. This is so even if the prohibited lifestyle or behavior is regarded negatively within the religion of the

---

right of religious school to dismiss unmarried teacher who became pregnant).

[70]*See, e.g., Cline v. Catholic Diocese of Toledo*, 206 F.3d 651, 666-68 (6th Cir. 2000) (reversing and remanding for factual determination concerning whether rule of sexual abstinence applied equally to men and women).

employer.[71] A lifestyle prohibition by the employer constitutes religious discrimination only if the employer takes the additional step of requiring employees to adopt the employer's religious convictions about the prohibited behavior.[72] If this is true for a secular employer, it necessarily follows that it is true for a religious employer. Reliance on 702(a) is not even required.

Consider the dismissal of an employee for stealing office supplies or for lying on a job application. The employee's discharge does not constitute religious discrimination, even if the employer holds a religious belief that "thou shalt not steal" or "thou shalt not bear false witness." Only if the employer requires employees to subscribe to the Eighth or Ninth Commandment as a matter of religious conviction would the dismissal constitute religious discrimination actionable under Title VII.

This illustration governs in the much more contentious circumstance where an employer's rules bear on an employee's extramarital sexual practices. Some employers, particularly faith-based organizations, are concerned that an employee's extramarital sexual behavior might not only result in diminished office morale or personnel disruption but also create a "public image" problem for the employer. Although these lifestyle cases make for eye-catching headlines in the popular press, the law is well settled that such cases do not even state a claim of religious discrimination.[73] This is so whether the employer is a secular organization or a religious

---

[71] The "employer" here is generally a small corporation or other small business and it is the owner's religion that matters. In other cases, an employee's supervisor may be imposing his or her religion.

[72] *Venters v. City of Delphi*, 123 F.3d 956 (7th Cir. 1997) (employee was lectured from the Bible, told she should attend church of employer's owner, and told to convert to avoid dismissal from employment); *Shapolia v. Los Alamos National Laboratory*, 992 F.2d 1033 (10th Cir. 1993) (Mormon supervisors said to have given negative job evaluation to employee because he was not a Mormon); *Blalock v. Metals Trades, Inc.*, 775 F.2d 703 (6th Cir. 1985) (employee laid off until he "got things straightened out" with spiritual leader of employer's owner).

[73] *See Hall v. Baptist Memorial Health Care Corp.*, 215 F.3d 618 (6th Cir. 2000) (counselor to student nurses at religious hospital lawfully discharged when it became known she was a lesbian; hospital did not try to tell employee where to attend church or what she had to believe concerning biblical teaching on homosexuality); *Pedreira v. Kentucky Baptist Homes for Children, Inc.*, 186 F. Supp.2d 757, 760-62

organization. Section 702(a) need not even be raised as a defense by a faith-based organization to have a lifestyle discrimination case dismissed.

This no-nonsense approach by the courts was borne out in the recent case of *Pedreira v. Kentucky Baptist Homes for Children, Inc.*[74] The plaintiff, discharged from her job as a youth counselor at a Baptist children's home because of her lesbian lifestyle, brought a discrimination case invoking Title VII's ban on religious discrimination. The plaintiff also invoked the Establishment Clause. As to the latter claim, the plaintiff's argument was that state funding of a religious foster-care provider, when juxtaposed with her discharge because homosexual practice is contrary to the Baptist faith, constituted an establishment of religion. Both the State of Kentucky and the Baptist Home were named as defendants.

The federal district court rejected both of these novel claims.[75] The Title VII claim failed because the Baptist Home did not try to force the plaintiff to adopt its biblical beliefs. The Establishment Clause failed because the clause is not about protecting lifestyle, it is about protecting religion. If a lifestyle claim brought under Title VII does not constitute religious discrimination, then a lifestyle claim brought under the Establishment Clause does not constitute religious discrimination.

The federal court's analysis ended there. The state's payment of social-service funding to the Baptist Home was an unrelated matter that the court did not consider. Nor should the matter of government funding have been considered. There is no constitutionally cognizable connection between plaintiff's discharge for reasons of homosexual practice and the state's funding of foster care delivered by independent-sector providers. We have

(W.D. Kty. 2001) (counselor to youth at religious residential care home lawfully discharged when it became known she was lesbian; religious home did not try to tell plaintiff what she had to believe concerning biblical teaching on homosexuality, thus home could enforce lifestyle rules consistent with its understanding of its Christian mission).

[74] 186 F. Supp.2d 757 (W.D. Kty. 2001).

[75] *Id.* at 763.

53

repeatedly encountered this legal rationale (i.e., the absence of a legal nexus) in the discussion above, in *Corporation of the Presiding Bishop v. Amos*, in the "Church Amendment" to the Hill-Burton Act, and in *Saucier v. Employment Security Department*.

3 *Religious Staffing Where a Nondiscrimination Clause is Embedded in the Federal Program Legislation*

We have seen that the basic federal civil rights employment law, Title VII of the Civil Rights Act of 1964, acknowledges in 702(a) the freedom of faith-based organizations to take religion into account in their employment decisions. Moreover, contrary to the critics, this freedom is not forfeited when a faith-based organization accepts government funds, nor does the freedom become unconstitutional and thus null. In this Chapter we move beyond Title VII, for there is more to federal civil rights compliance than Title VII and, strictly speaking, 702(a) is applicable only to cases brought under Title VII. Furthermore, whereas Title VII is binding only when an employer has 15 or more employees, other federal nondiscrimination laws become applicable whenever the employer is a recipient of federal financial assistance.

All employers that receive federal financial assistance, including religious organizations, are subject to four additional federal civil rights statutes. However, because none of these four civil rights laws prohibit discrimination on the basis of religion, the statutes[76] do not implicate the right of religious staffing. So we proceed to take up the instance of federal social-service programs that include a statutory provision prohibiting employment discrimination on the basis of religion.

Almost all funding awards from the federal government to independent-sector organizations to provide social services take the form of a "grant" or "cooperative agreement" rather than a federal "contract."[77] Contracts are normally used by the federal government only to obtain goods or services for its own direct use—for example, research, janitorial services, or jet planes—as opposed to meeting the needs of members of society. However, occasionally a federal agency, such as the Bureau of Prisons, does enter into contracts for the purchase of social services.

---

[76]These statutes prohibit discrimination by the recipients of the federal financial assistance and apply regardless of the number of employees at the organization. Protected from discrimination are the beneficiaries of the funded program or activity. The four federal statutes are Title VI of the Civil Rights Act of 1964, 42 U.S.C. § 2000d *et seq.*, which prohibits discrimination on the bases of race, color, and national origin; the Age Discrimination Act of 1975, 29 U.S.C. §§ 6101-07, which prohibits discrimination on the basis of age; Section 504 of the Rehabilitation Act of 1973, 29 U.S.C. § 794, which prohibits discrimination against otherwise qualified individuals with disabilities; and finally, Title IX of the Educational Amendments of 1972, 20 U.S.C. §§ 1681-88, which prohibits discrimination on the bases of sex and visual impairment by educational institutions.

Additionally, two of these civil rights statutes have been construed to prohibit discrimination against the recipient's employees while the employees are working in the government-funded program. Title IX has been found to cover employment discrimination on the basis of sex. *North Haven Bd. of Educ. v. Bell,* 456 U.S. 512 (1982). However, religious educational institutions are exempt from the sex discrimination prohibition in Title IX if its application "would not be consistent with the religious tenets of such organization." 20 U.S.C. § 1681(a)(3). Section 504 has been found to cover employment discrimination on the basis of disability. *Consolidated Rail Corp. v. Darrone,* 465 U.S. 624 (1984); 45 C.F.R. § 84.11(a)(1).

Not every operation, division, or office of a funded recipient is covered by these four statutes, but faith-based organizations are well advised to take into account that "program or activity" is broadly defined. The definition of "program or activity" appears in Title VI, 42 U.S.C. § 2000d-4a. On the expanded coverage over federal grant recipients, including religious organizations, as a result of the Civil Rights Restoration Act of 1987, see Carl H. Esbeck, *The Regulation of Religious Organizations As Recipients of Governmental Assistance* 29-33 (1996). "Federal financial assistance" is also broadly defined and includes grants, loans, and in☐kind transfers of goods or services, but does not include tax credits or tax exemptions. *Id.* at 28.

[77]The three terms are defined at 31 U.S.C. §§ 6301-08.

For a number of years, pursuant to presidential executive order, the rules for federal contracting restricted religious staffing.[78] These rules never applied to the bulk of federal social spending, which involves grants or cooperative agreements, not contracts. However, in late 2002 the federal contracting rules were brought into line with 702(a) and, hence, with the religious staffing freedom generally.[79] Now all faith-based organizations that enter into contracts with the federal government, whether to provide services to the government itself or to others, are free to staff on a religious basis.

A. Program-Specific Nondiscrimination Clauses in Federal Legislation

Some federal social-service programs have a nondiscrimination provision embedded in their implementing statutes. While this is true of only a minority of all federal social programs, still the number of such embedded provisions is not insubstantial. The principal thrust of these provisions is to prohibit discrimination against the intended beneficiaries of the funded programs. However, a few of these embedded clauses expressly prohibit employment discrimination by a service provider against its employees. In still other statutes the provision prohibits discrimination against the intended beneficiaries of the funded social services, but "beneficiaries" has been interpreted broadly in the courts also to prohibit discrimination by a provider against its employees.[80]

---

[78]Executive Order 11246, 30 Fed. Reg. 12319 (Sept. 24, 1965).

[79]Executive Order 13279 § 4, 67 Fed. Reg. 77141, 77143 (Dec. 16, 2002). The Executive Order is reprinted in Appendix 6.

[80]Some federal programs, such as the Community Development Block Grant program and the Head Start program, include civil rights language requiring that no one will be denied program benefits or be discriminated against on account of their race, color, national origin, sex, or religion. CDBG, 42 U.S.C. § 5309; Head Start, 42 U.S.C. § 9849(a). Although this additional language does not mention employment, a White House report notes that "some older U.S. Supreme Court cases indicate that these statutes may also apply to employment decisions." White House Office of Faith-Based and Community Initiatives, *Protecting the Civil Rights and Religious Liberty of Faith-Based Organizations: Why*

These "embedded" employment nondiscrimination provisions are presumptively binding on all recipients of federal funds awarded under those programs. Examples are found in the Workforce Investment Act of 1998,[81] administered by the U.S. Department of Labor, and the first title of the Omnibus Crime Control and Safe Streets Act of 1968,[82] administered by the U.S. Department of Justice. An embedded provision, if it covers employees as well as beneficiaries, prohibits discrimination against a recipient's employees only while the employees are working in the government-funded program. Two programs, AmeriCorps VISTA and AmeriCorps State and National, both operated by the Corporation for National and Community Service, have an embedded clause restricting religious staffing, but the restriction is limited to new staff hired with the federal program funds.[83]

B. The Religious Freedom Restoration Act of 1993

Where these "embedded" nondiscrimination clauses apply to federally assisted social-service providers, faith-based organizations that employ staff on a religious basis may turn to the Religious Freedom Restoration Act of 1993[84] (RFRA) for protection.[85] RFRA excuses federally funded faith-based

---

Religious Hiring Rights Must Be Preserved 5-6 (June 23, 2003); *available at* <http://www. whitehouse.gov/government/fbci /booklet.pdf>; *reprinted in* Appendix 8.

[81] 29 U.S.C. § 2801 *et seq.* Sec. 2938(a)(2), prohibits discrimination on several bases, including religion.

[82] 42 U.S.C. § 3711 *et seq.* Sec. 3789d(c)(1), prohibits discrimination on several bases, including religion.

[83] 42 U.S.C. § 12635(c)(1) and (2).

[84] 42 U.S.C. §§ 2000bb to 2000bb-4.

[85] The White House Office of Faith-Based and Community Initiatives advises faith-based organizations that, notwithstanding restrictive statutory language in some federal funding programs, faith-based organizations may resort to RFRA for protection. *See* White House Office of Faith-Based and Community Initiatives, *Protecting the Civil Rights and Religious Liberty of Faith-Based Organizations: Why Religious Hiring Rights Must Be Preserved* 4 n.3, 5 n.4 (June 23, 2003), *available at* <http://www .whitehouse.gov/government/fbci/booklet.pdf>; *reprinted in* Appendix 8. Further, the regulations for

organizations[86] from having to incur a substantial religious burden when the burden is imposed by a generally applicable federal law.[87]

Being prohibited from staffing on a religious basis is most assuredly a burden on the free exercise of religion. It is no answer to argue, as some opponents of the faith-based initiative do, that a religious organization can easily avoid the burden by simply forgoing the competition for a grant. Just as the government cannot justify restricting a particular form of speech (e.g., passing out handbills on a public street) merely by pointing to other opportunities that a person has to express herself (e.g., writing a letter to the editor of a newspaper), so the government cannot restrict a particular exercise of religion by pointing to another course of action where the organization's religious practices are not penalized.

In any event, the question is free of serious doubt because RFRA explicitly states that a "denial of government funding" on account of a

---

several of the Substance Abuse and Mental Health Services Administration's (SAMHSA) drug-abuse prevention and treatment programs appeal to RFRA to nullify a statutory limitation on faith-based recipients of the funding. *Charitable Choice Regulations Applicable to States Receiving Substance Abuse Prevention and Treatment Block Grants, Projects for Assistance in Transition From Homelessness Formula Grants, and to Public and Private Providers Receiving Discretionary Grant Funding From SAMHSA for the Provision of Substance Abuse Services Providing for Equal Treatment of SAMHSA Program Participants*, 68 Fed. Reg. 56430, 56435 (Sept. 30, 2003); *excerpted in* Appendix 5. The final rule for the Department of Justice's Equal Treatment regulations notes that RFRA applies even though it is not specifically mentioned in the regulations. *Participation in Justice Department Programs by Religious Organizations; Providing for Equal Treatment of All Justice Department Program Participants*, 69 Fed. Reg. 2836 (Jan. 21, 2004); *excerpted in* Appendix 7. The final rule for the Department of Health and Human Service's Equal Treatment regulations includes a similar comment. *Participation in Department of Health and Human Services Programs by Religious Organizations; Providing for Equal Treatment of All Department of Health and Human Services Program Participants*, 69 Fed. Reg. 42591 (July 16, 2004).

[86]RFRA reads in terms of protecting the rights of "persons," but under the U.S. Code the term "persons" includes organizations, thereby including protection for faith-based organizations. *See* 1 U.S.C. § 1.

[87]In one sense RFRA is case-specific, responding to each individual's or organization's sincerely held claim of religious burden. But for faith-based organizations that staff on a religious basis RFRA will always grant relief from generally applicable employment laws prohibiting discrimination on the basis of religion. Because RFRA will grant relief without fail to faith-based organizations with sincerely held religious staffing practices, it is correct to suggest, as we have in the text, that there is a presumption that RFRA excuses faith-based organizations from the religious burden imposed by these program-embedded nondiscrimination provisions. As with any presumption, the government, of course, can inquire into the bona fides of the faith-based organization's claim and rebut the operation of RFRA by evidence of insincerity.

service provider's religion or religious practice can trigger RFRA.[88] This is only logical. Congress enacted RFRA to "restore" the standard of protection for religious free exercise reflected in *Sherbert v. Verner*,[89] a case about a denial of government funding.[90] The Supreme Court held in *Sherbert* that an individual refusing to take a job entailing work on her Sabbath could not be put to the "cruel choice" either to forfeit her claim for unemployment benefits or to violate her religious day-of-rest. Likewise, a faith-based organization cannot be put to the "cruel choice" either to forfeit its ability to compete for valuable federal grant monies or to violate its religious practice of employing only those of like-minded faith.

In RFRA itself the term "religious exercise" is broadly defined to include "any exercise of religion, whether or not compelled by, or central to, a system of religious belief."[91] Nonetheless, opponents further argue that for government to decline to facilitate the free exercise of religion is not a "religious" burden. It is true, of course, that the Free Exercise Clause is written in terms of what the government cannot do to a faith-based organization and not in terms of what a faith-based organization can exact from the government. But that line of argumentation does not describe what is occurring here. The government may indeed choose to deliver all social

---

[88] *See* 42 U.S.C. § 2000bb-4 ("Granting government funding . . . shall not constitute a violation of this chapter. As used in this section, the term 'granting,' used with respect to government funding, . . . does not include the denial of government funding . . . "). *See also* Senate Report No. 103-111, at 13 ("parties may challenge, under the Religious Freedom Restoration Act, the denial of benefits to themselves as in *Sherber[t]*"); *id.* at 15 ("the denial of [government] funding . . . may constitute a violation of the act, as was the case under the free exercise clause in *Sherbert v. Verner*"). Senate Report No. 103-111 is reprinted at 1993 U.S.C.C.A.N. 1892.

[89] 374 U.S. 398 (1963).

[90] RFRA states, as one of its purposes, "to restore the compelling interest test" of *Sherbert v. Verner*. 42 U.S.C. § 2000bb(b)(1). The denial of funding in *Sherbert* was slightly different from the denial of a social-service grant to a faith-based organization. But RFRA was not drafted to restore the holding of a single case. *Sherbert* was illustrative of the problem, not the whole problem. The terms of RFRA read in general principles, with the object being the provision of a remedy for a variety of religious burdens—no matter how or where the burdens occur.

[91] 42 U.S.C. § 2000bb-2(4) (incorporating by reference the definition of "religious exercise" in 42 U.S.C. § 2000cc-5(7)).

services by itself. In such a circumstance, the fact that a faith-based provider cannot win a grant is not a free exercise burden.[92] The federal government, however, has not chosen such a path. Instead, almost all government social services are delivered by the independent sector. Having chosen to deliver services through providers in the independent sector, the federal government cannot then pick and choose among those available providers using eligibility criteria that have a discriminatory impact on faith-based providers. A religious discriminatory impact from an otherwise neutral law is the very type of occurrence that Congress sought to halt by enacting RFRA.[93]

Conceding, as they must, that by its terms a denial of grant funding can trigger RFRA protection, opponents of the faith-based initiative argue that RFRA cannot be invoked by a religious provider because the loss of grant monies is not a "substantial" religious burden.[94] This makes no sense. It is true that religious organizations making claims of increased financial burden, without more, have not been excused from compliance with general regulatory and tax legislation.[95] That is, it is not enough simply to show that a neutral law increases a faith-based provider's costs of operation. But such cases have no resemblance to the claim of burden here. Instead, the statutory restriction on religious staffing uniquely harms faith-based organizations by preventing them from maintaining their religious character

---

[92] In *Brusca v. Board of Education*, 405 U.S. 1050 (1972) (decision below summarily aff'd), the Supreme Court affirmed that a state's provision of free public school education only does not compel the state to provide an equal benefit to religious school parents. *Luetkemeyer v. Kaufmann*, 419 U.S. 888 (1974) (decision below summarily aff'd), likewise affirmed that a state may choose to provide free bussing to government schools alone without providing an equal benefit to religious schools. But *Brusca* and *Luetkemeyer* are inapposite to the situation here where the government has elected to involve private charities in the delivery of social services.

[93] *See* 42 U.S.C. § 2000bb-1(a) ("Government shall not substantially burden a person's exercise of religion even if the burden results from a rule of general applicability").

[94] As part of the *prima facie* case, RFRA requires proof of a substantial burden on a claimant's religion. 42 U.S.C. § 2000bb-1(a) and (b).

[95] *See, e.g., Jimmy Swaggart Ministries v. California Bd. of Equalization*, 493 U.S. 378 (1990) (upholding uniform state levy of sales and use taxes on sale of religious material).

by hiring only co-religionists. The harm is not financial or increased operating costs, the harm is religious.[96] A prohibition on religious staffing cuts the very soul out of a faith-based organization's ability to define and pursue its spiritual calling, as well as its ability to sustain its vision over generations.

RFRA itself can be overridden, of course, upon proof by the federal government of a "compelling governmental interest."[97] But it is absurd to claim, as a few opponents do, that the eradication of religious staffing by faith-based organizations is a compelling interest. Congress sought to achieve just the opposite when it provided in 702(a) that Title VII's ban on religious discrimination should not apply to religious organizations. Permitting religious charities to staff on a religious basis does not undermine compelling social norms or constitutional values. Just the opposite is true. This freedom minimizes the influence of government actions on the religious choices of both beneficiaries and religious providers. Safeguarding a faith-based organization's freedom of religious staffing advances the Establishment Clause value of noninterference by government in religious affairs. Senator Sam Ervin said it more colorfully when he stated that the aim of the staffing freedom was to "take the political hands of Caesar off the institutions of God, where they have no place to be." In *Corporation of the Presiding Bishop v. Amos*, the Supreme Court put its seal of approval on that congressional judgment.[98]

Moreover, siding with religious freedom is the judgment not just of

---

[96] The dollar amount, large or small, of any particular available grant is not relevant to RFRA's "substantial burden" requirement. A promise to comply with these program-embedded employment nondiscrimination provisions is an essential criteria of grant eligibility. Not to accommodate sincerely held religious employment practices is thus a categorical bar, from here to eternity, to a faith-based organization's eligibility for any such federal grant program. That unquestionably is a substantial burden or "cruel choice," and the burden is uniquely religious rather than monetary.

[97] 42 U.S.C. § 2000bb-1(b).

[98] *Amos*, 483 U.S. at 332 n.9 (1987).

Congress in 702(a) and a unanimous Court in *Amos*, but also of President
Bush as he spoke while instituting his Administration's faith-based
initiative:

> We will encourage faith-based and community programs
> without changing their mission. We will help all in their work to
> change hearts while keeping a commitment to pluralism . . . .
>
> Government has important responsibilities for public health or
> public order and civil rights . . . . Yet when we see social needs in
> America, my administration will look first to faith-based programs
> and community groups, which have proven their power to save
> and change lives. We will not fund the religious activities of any
> group. But when people of faith provide social services, we will
> not discriminate against them.
>
> As long as there are secular alternatives, faith-based charities
> should be able to compete for funding on an equal basis, and in a
> manner that does not cause them to sacrifice their mission.[99]

The President's speech has all the right elements: effective help for the
poor as the paramount concern, equality among providers without regard to
religion or ideology, and respect for civil rights within a framework that
values everyone equally and thereby does not force a change in the
religious mission of charities that serve out of faith. Lastly, it has been
widely observed that protecting the religious character of faith-based
organizations that participate in government programs expands the choices
available to the poor and needy, some of whom desire to seek out assistance
at robustly faith-centered providers.[100]

---

[99]Remarks by the President in Announcement of the Faith-Based Initiative (Jan. 29, 2001), *available at*
<http://www.whitehouse.gov/news/releases/print/20010129-5.html>.

[100]*See* 105th Cong., 2d Sess., 144 Cong Rec., S12686, S12687 (Oct. 20, 1998) (statement of John D.
Ashcroft on Charitable Choice) ("Demanding that religious ministries 'secularize' in order to qualify to
be a government-funded provider of services hurts intended beneficiaries of social services, as it
eliminates a fuller range of provider choices for the poor and needy, frustrating those beneficiaries with
spiritual interests.").

Diversity is expanded, not diminished, when the government affirms the equality of all independent-sector providers to participate in social-service programs without privileging any particular ideology. By the same token, this neutral approach permits communities of ultimate meaning to preserve the institutional character necessary to perpetuate their distinctive way of life. These are the social norms to be upheld and the constitutional values to be reinforced. In the face of these affirmations from all three branches of the federal government, the opponents' bald assertion that a ban on religious staffing holds the high ground of "social norm" are little more than self-flattery.

We hasten to remind readers that reliance on RFRA in no way excuses compliance with federal civil rights laws when it comes to employment discrimination on the basis of race, color, national origin, sex, age, or disability. RFRA guards only against burdens on religion.[101] Moreover, RFRA does not excuse compliance with the operation of state and local laws, only compliance with federal laws and the actions of federal officials.[102] It is the matter of state and local laws that we now take up.

---

[101] Opponents argue that using RFRA to overcome embedded program restrictions on religious staffing would excuse racial discrimination rooted in religious belief. Not true. We have seen no RFRA case where racial discrimination was excused under the guise of religion, and in any event the Supreme Court has already held that the denial of benefits to a religious organization in the interest of eradicating racial discrimination is a compelling governmental interest. *See Bob Jones Univ. v. United States*, 461 U.S. 574, 602-04, 604 n.29 (1983). RFRA claims are overridden, of course, by compelling governmental interests. 42 U.S.C. § 2000bb-1(b).

[102] *City of Boerne v. Flores*, 521 U.S. 507 (1997) (holding that RFRA cannot be applied to the actions of state or local governments).

4   *The Religious Staffing Freedom Where Federal Funds Pass Through State and Local Governments*

The majority of all federal funds for social services are distributed initially to state and local governments and only thereafter are awarded to providers in the independent sector. Often the federal programs require state and local governments to add their own matching funds, and sometime they voluntarily add money of their own to the federal funds. All of the state and local funds commingled with the federal funds are subject to the rules of the federal social-service program.[103]

When the federal monies go first to a state or local government and only thereafter are awarded to independent-sector providers, then the application of state and local laws must be considered. It is common for state and local governments, when they purchase social services, to have

---

[103]Required matching funds (sometimes called maintenance-of-effort (MOE) funds), as well as any voluntarily added funds added to the program budget or otherwise commingled with federal funds, enlarge the applicability of Charitable Choice and hence enlarge the religious staffing freedom. For example, the regulations applicable to the TANF program provide that Charitable Choice applies not only to the federal funds but also to state commingled funds expended pursuant to a state's maintenance-of-effort (MOE) requirement. *Charitable Choice Provisions Applicable to the Temporary Assistance for Needy Families Program*, 68 Fed. Reg. 56449, 56450, 56462-63, 56465-66 (Sept. 30, 2003); *excerpted in* Appendix 4.

"procurement" laws (also called "purchasing" or "contracting" laws) that bind independent-sector recipients of these monies—even with regard to grant monies that originated with the federal government.

Most of these procurement laws deal with the proper accounting and use of program funds. However, procurement laws in some state and local jurisdictions prohibit employment discrimination on various bases, including religion. Some of these jurisdictions include an exemption for religious organizations, but others do not. If a religious charity receives federal funds by way of such a state or local government that has an employment nondiscrimination procurement law, then the question arises whether the charity has lost the freedom to staff on a religious basis.

As we shall see below, if the federal funds are subject to the rules of Charitable Choice, then the religious charity's freedom to staff on a religious basis is retained. However, before turning to a discussion of these procurement laws, we need to become acquainted with employment nondiscrimination laws that arise out of a state's "police power."

A. State and Local "Police Power" Legislation

Nearly every state has a human rights act that prohibits employment discrimination.[104] These state acts impose employment nondiscrimination duties in addition to any already imposed by Title VII of the 1964 Civil Rights Act or other federal civil rights acts.[105] Human rights acts derive from the "police power" of a state. Police power is a state's authority to

---

[104] *See Topical Index – Religious Discrimination – State,* Employment Practices Guide (CCH) Vol. 1, p. 79 (cross-referencing to statutes in the states and the District of Columbia); Peter M. Panken, et al., *A State-by-State Survey of the Law on Religion in the Workplace* (2001) (compilation of laws of the 50 states and the District of Columbia). One recent survey reports that 46 states have comprehensive employment nondiscrimination laws. *See* Ira C. Lupu and Robert W. Tuttle, *Government Partnerships with Faith-Based Service Providers: The State of the Law* 47 (Roundtable on Religion and Social Welfare Policy, December 2002); *available at* <http://www.religionandsocialpolicy.org/docs/legal/reports/12-4-2002_state_of_the_law.pdf>.

[105] *See* 42 U.S.C. § 2000e-7.

legislate on behalf of the health, safety, morals, or general welfare of the state's citizens and others within its borders. Thus, these laws apply irrespective of whether there is funding or other financial assistance from the state government. Municipalities and counties can also enact similar nondiscrimination ordinances if the state legislature has delegated to the local governmental body the authority to regulate concerning employment discrimination.[106]

Human rights acts vary from state to state. For example, one state's act may apply to employers with as few as one employee whereas another state's act applies only to employers with 15 or more employees.[107] Discrimination in employment is typically prohibited on the basis of race, color, national origin, sex, or religion. Some states have included age, disability, marital status, and the like, as prohibited bases. Eleven states and the District of Columbia presently prohibit employment discrimination on the basis of sexual orientation. Many municipalities and counties, typically those with larger populations, have also adopted employment nondiscrimination ordinances that include sexual orientation.[108]

Religious organizations, as employers, are generally subject to these state human rights acts and local governmental ordinances, the same as any other employer. However, as with Title VII of the Civil Rights Act of 1964, religion is different. Almost without fail these state acts and local ordinances either exempt religious organizations from the prohibition on religious staffing, define covered "employers" so as to exclude religious

---

[106]On occasion, municipal employment nondiscrimination ordinances have been overturned because the state had not delegated to the local municipality or county the authority to adopt such an ordinance. *See Arlington County v. White*, 528 S.E.2d 706 (Va. 2000).

[107]*See* Paul Taylor, *The Costs of Denying Religious Organizations the Right to Staff on a Religious Basis When They Join Federal Social Service Efforts*, George Mason University Civil Rights Law Journal, 12 (2002): 159, 170 n.41 (collecting human rights acts from every state and indicating their scope of coverage).

[108]For the most current information, see the web page of Lambda Defense League, <http://www. lambdalegal.org>.

discrimination by religious organizations, or provide religious organizations with a "bona fide occupational qualification" defense for religious staffing in jobs with religious duties.[109] Thus, with rare exceptions, the religious staffing freedom is unimpaired by these acts.

With respect to discrimination on other prohibited bases, such as sex, sexual orientation, or marital status, these state and local laws generally must be followed by religious organizations—subject to constitutional defenses.[110] A religious charity wanting to avoid the application of these state and local laws can cease doing business in the jurisdiction. Of course, that option is more realistic when the offending jurisdiction is a municipality or county rather than an entire state.

Because these police power laws, almost without fail, acknowledge the religious staffing freedom, we now take up procurement laws, which are far more problematic.

B. State and Local Procurement Legislation

State and local governments award funds to nongovernmental providers by various means, such as grants, contracts, or vouchers. The applicable procurement laws, unlike the police power laws discussed above, have their

---

[109] See the references in footnote 104, above.

[110] Constitutional defenses raised by faith-based organizations have been found to override state and local civil rights laws prohibiting discrimination on the bases of sexual orientation and marital status. See Madsen v. Erwin, 395 Mass. 715, 481 N.E.2d 1160 (1985) (sexual orientation claim dismissed); Walker v. First Presbyterian Church, 22 Fair Empl. Prac. Cas. (BNA) 762, 23 Empl. Prac. Dec. (CCH) ¶ 31,006 (Cal. Super. 1980) (sexual orientation claim dismissed); Arriaga v. Loma Linda University, 10 Cal. App. 4th 1556, 13 Cal. Rptr.2d 619 (1992) (marital status claim dismissed). Similarly, the religious freedom defenses raised by landlords have been found to override laws prohibiting discrimination on the basis of marital status where the lawsuit is brought by cohabiting couples. See McCready v. Hoffius, 586 N.W.2d 723 (Mich. 1998), vacated in part on other grounds, 593 N.W.2d 545 (Mich. 1999), summary judgment granted, No. 94-69472 slip op. (Cir. Ct. for Jackson Cty., Mich., Dec. 6, 2000) (marital status claim dismissed); Attorney General v. Desilets, 636 N.E. 2d 233 (Mass. 1994) (marital status claim vacated and remanded); Cooper v. French, 460 N.W.2d 2 (Minn. 1990) (marital status claim dismissed). See also Boy Scouts of America v. Dale, 530 U.S. 640 (2000) (free speech and freedom of association rights of voluntary membership organization devoted to youth character development override state gay rights law).

authority in the government's spending power. Hence, procurement laws apply only when accompanied by funds within the spending authority of the state or local government.[111] These are the metaphorical "strings" that come attached to the government dollar.

Although procurement laws are primarily concerned with proper accounting and use of funds, it is not uncommon for these laws also to require employment nondiscrimination by those in the independent sector that are recipients of the funds.

Such requirements, where they occur, typically apply without regard to the number of an organization's employees. Instead, they apply to procurement agreements over a certain amount, say $25,000. These procurement laws typically prohibit discrimination on the basis of race, color, national origin, sex, or religion, and increasingly also on the bases of age, disability, marital status, sexual orientation, and the like. When it comes to a religious organization discriminating on the basis of religion, there might be an express exemption. But it is not uncommon that there is no exemption written into the text of the procurement law.[112]

When a charitable organization is a recipient of federal social-service funds by way of a state or local government, then these state and local procurement laws are presumptively binding on the provider. When the

---

[111] It is common for states not to share federal welfare monies with local governments. Where this is so, then local governmental procurement rules never come into play. For example, as to the $16.5 billion in federal TANF funds received each year by the states in block grants, in 24 states all contracts with independent-sector welfare providers occur at the state level. In five states the contracting occurs entirely at the local governmental level, and in 20 states contracts are awarded at both levels. Government Accounting Office, *WELFARE REFORM: Interim Report on Potential Ways to Strengthen Federal Oversight of State and Local Contracting* 8 (GAO-02-245, April 2002).

[112] *See* Paul Taylor, *The Costs of Denying Religious Organizations the Right to Staff on a Religious Basis When They Join Federal Social Service Efforts*, 12 George Mason University Civil Rights Law Journal 159, 196 n.128 (2002) (collecting procurement laws from eleven states that prohibit religious discrimination); Ira C. Lupu and Robert W. Tuttle, *State-by-State Summary of Religious Exemption Statues (Appendix B)*, in GOVERNMENT PARTNERSHIPS WITH FAITH-BASED SERVICE PROVIDERS: THE STATE OF THE LAW (Roundtable on Religion and Social Welfare Policy, December 2002), *available at* <http://www. religionandsocialpolicy.org/docs/legal/reports/12-4-2002_ state_of_the_law.pdf>; and the

provider is a faith-based organization, the question arises concerning whether the organization has lost the right to staff on a religious basis. That is the question before us in the balance of this chapter.

State and local procurement laws must not be inconsistent with federal law,[113] including constitutional defenses. The Supremacy Clause of the federal Constitution resolves any inconsistency or conflict in favor of federal law.[114] If the federal funds are subject to Charitable Choice, then the faith-based organization's freedom to staff on a religious basis is preserved. This is true because, as explained below, Charitable Choice was adopted in Congress with the understanding that it protects religious staffing and thus overrides any state and local procurement law to the contrary. The picture is less clear when dealing with federal funds under programs not subject to Charitable Choice.

1. Federal Social-Service Funds Subject to the Safeguards of Charitable Choice

Congress has provided Charitable Choice safeguards for the religious hiring practices of faith-based organizations that receive government funds from the TANF welfare program, the Community Services Block Grant (CSBG) program, and several SAMHSA programs that fund substance-

---

web page of Lambda Defense League, <http://www.lambdalegal.org>.

[113] *See, e.g., Air Transport Ass'n of America v. City and County of San Francisco*, 992 F. Supp. 1149 (N.D. Cal. 1998), *aff'd and remanded*, 266 F.3d 1064 (9th Cir. 2001) (holding by trial court that federal ERISA conflicted with, and thereby preempted, city's domestic partner benefits plan).

[114] For example, Congress recently passed a law that supersedes an ordinance of the District of Columbia. Congress wanted to preserve the religious staffing freedom for K-12 religious schools, and that necessitated preempting a local ordinance. Congress provided for school vouchers which parents could use at participating private schools, including religious schools. However, D.C. had a procurement ordinance that prohibited employment discrimination on the bases of religion and sexual orientation. Accordingly many religious schools would not take the vouchers unless the ordinance was preempted. The D.C. School Choice Incentive Act of 2003, Pub. L. No. 108-199, 118 Stat. 126, 130-31 (Jan. 23, 2004), does just that. Section 308(d)(1) provides as follows: "Notwithstanding any other provision of law, a school participating in any program under this title that is operated by, supervised by, controlled by, or connected to, a religious organization may exercise its right in matters of employment consistent

abuse treatment and prevention services.

Charitable Choice overrules state and local employment nondiscrimination procurement rules that would otherwise prohibit religious staffing.[115] This was done statutorily by Congress in order to preserve the religious independence of faith-based organizations and thereby encourage these providers to compete for federal social-service funding.[116]

The first Charitable Choice provision, enacted in August 1996, was

---

with title VII of the Civil Rights Act of 1964, including the exemptions in such title." The "notwithstanding any other law" phrase thereby preempts the D.C. ordinance when contrary to a religious school's religious staffing—a right consistent with the staffing freedom acknowledged in 702(a) of Title VII.

[115]The White House Office of Faith-Based and Community Initiatives, in discussing the funding streams that are subject to Charitable Choice protections, has the following guidance: "These laws also provide that faith-based organizations that receive Federal funds may continue to carry out their missions consistent with their beliefs. For example, they may maintain a religious environment in their facilities, and they may consider their religious beliefs in hiring and firing employees." White House Office of Faith-Based and Community Initiatives, *Guidance to Faith-Based and Community Organizations on Partnering with the Federal Government* 12 (Dec. 12, 2002), *available at* <http://www.whitehouse.gov/government/fbci /guidance_document.pdf>; *see also* White House Office of Faith-Based and Community Initiatives, Executive Office of the President, *Protecting the Civil Rights and Religious Liberty of Faith-Based Organizations: Why Religious Hiring Rights Must Be Preserved* 4 (June 23, 2003), *available at* <http://www.whitehouse.gov/ government/fbci/booklet.pdf>, *reprinted in* Appendix 8; and David M. Ackerman, *Public Aid to Faith-Based Organizations (Charitable Choice) in the 107th Congress: Background and Selected Legal Issues,* Congressional Research Service Report for Congress, order code RL31043, 32-33 (Aug. 19, 2003).

[116]Charitable Choice has preemption prevention (i.e., "saving") language in 42 U.S.C. § 604a(k), but the subsection does not affect the religious staffing freedom. Subsection (k) is of limited scope for two reasons. First, subsection (k) pertains only to "saving" certain state laws from preemption, not local governmental ordinances. If Congress had meant for subsection (k) to "save" from preemption local ordinances along with certain state laws, then Congress would have expressly referenced local governments. *See, e.g.,* 42 U.S.C. § 604a(d)(1) (using phrase "shall retain its independence from Federal, State, and local governments" when Congress means to include local ordinances). The Charitable Choice provisions are reprinted in Appendix 3. This differing treatment of state and local procurement rules is reflected in HHS regulations concerning the Substance Abuse and Mental Health Services Administration. *Compare* 45 C.F.R. § 92.36(a) *with* § 92.36(b)(1).

Second, what little legislative history we have concerning subsection (k) shows that the subsection was targeted on Blaine Amendments. Blaine Amendments are state constitutional provisions that expressly prohibit state government from aiding religion and religious organizations. *See* Conf. Rept. No. 430, accompanying H.R. 4, 104th Cong., 1st Sess., 361 (Dec. 20, 1995). This 1995 Conference Report gives an account of a congressionally adopted welfare reform bill with the identical subsection (k). Although the 1995 bill was vetoed by President Clinton, a follow-up federal welfare reform act, with the same codified at 42 U.S.C. § 604a and served as the model for later provisions.[117] Subsection (b) (§ 604a(b)), states that one of the overarching congressional purposes of Charitable Choice is that religious charities be equally eligible for federal grant funds "without impairing the religious character of such organizations." Congress thus intended religious organizations to retain the level of religious autonomy they enjoyed before becoming recipients of federal funds. Subsection (d) (§ 604a(d)) provides substance to that congressional purpose. Subsection (d)(1) says that a faith-based organization "shall retain its independence from Federal, State, and local governments, including such organization's control over the definition, development, practice, and expression of its religious beliefs." Furthermore, subsection (d)(2)(A) specifically provides that faith-based organizations need not alter their form of "internal governance," which surely includes the hiring, supervision, discipline, and discharge of officers and other governing personnel.

Preemption thus occurs with regard to state and local nondiscrimination procurement laws, but only when those laws are inimical to the religious provider's "religious character" or religious "independence." The word "retain" in subsection (d)(1) is pivotal. For a faith-based organization to "retain" its "independence" from "Federal, State, and local governments" means that the level of religious independence a faith-based organization had before it applied for and was awarded Charitable Choice monies is not to be diminished (or enlarged). That is, the religious organization is not to suffer a net reduction in religious autonomy as a result of taking

---

subsection (k), was enacted in August 1996. Based on the Conference Report, avoiding the application of a Blaine Amendment is possible by keeping the federal program funds separate from state funds. Because Blaine Amendments would frustrate the federal policy behind Charitable Choice, Congress desires states to let the federal rules operate unimpeded. Thus, where state funds are commingled with federal funds the federal rules apply and any Blaine Amendments are preempted. "Charitable Choice Provisions Applicable to the Temporary Assistance for Needy Families Program," 68 Fed. Reg. 56449, 56463 (Sept. 30, 2003); *excerpted in* Appendix 4. Additionally, where state and federal funds are commingled, subsection (k) does not "save" from preemption state employment nondiscrimination procurement laws. *Id.*

[117]Section 604a is reprinted in Appendix 3.

government money that is subject to Charitable Choice.

Police power laws apply to organizations in a jurisdiction whether or not the organizations receive government funding, and thus police power restrictions on religious staffing are left unchanged by subsection (d)(1). However, Congress sought to prevent state and local governments from attaching procurement "strings" to federal funds by means of their procurement laws when such procurement "strings" undermine a faith-based organization's "religious character" or "independence." Without such a promise, many religious providers would simply "sit out" the faith-based initiative. As a consequence, the congressional attempt to draw increased numbers of religious organizations into being part of the nation's social safety net would fail.

It is the overarching congressional purpose in subsection (b), backed up by the substantive rules of subsection (d), that lays down the federal rule or standard for preemption. Of course, when enacting Charitable Choice, Congress could not anticipate every situation where a procurement law would undermine a faith-based organization's religious autonomy. Congress thus did the next best thing by setting down an explicit standard. When a faith-based organization has a sincere religious belief concerning religious staffing, subsections (b), (d)(1), and (d)(2)(A), collectively, override conflicting state and local procurement laws.[118]

If these Charitable Choice subsections did not preempt conflicting

---

[118]Opponents of the faith-based initiative have known for some time that Charitable Choice preempts state and local procurement laws that would otherwise prohibit a faith-based organization from staffing on a religious basis. They opposed the expansion of Charitable Choice for that reason. For example, when H.R. 7 was debated in the House Judiciary Committee in June 2001, and on the House floor in July 2001, the subsection (d) language was understood by both Majority and Dissenting Views as overriding state and local employment nondiscrimination laws. *See, e.g.,* House Committee on the Judiciary, *Community Solutions Act of 2001,* H.R. 7, REPT. NO. 107-138, 107th Cong., 1st Sess. Part I, 37-38, 176, 249-54, 258-66 (majority views), p. 290 n.7 (minority views), *available at* <http://www.house.gov /judiciary/107-138p1.pdf>. See also a letter of April 9, 2003, from Rep. Barney Frank to Attorney General John Ashcroft admitting that "it was generally assumed by all parties in the debate on H.R. 7 that the similar language in that bill would have had the effect of pre-empting inconsistent state and local laws." <http://www. house.gov/frank/faithbased2003.html>. Similarly, Charitable Choice opponents in Congress argued against various bills because of the preemption of state

procurement laws, then the language of subsection (d) seemingly would have little or no application. To render congressional language a nullity is contrary to the canon of statutory construction that all legislative words are to be given meaning if it is at all reasonable to do so. In the 1996 federal welfare reform law, the chief application of Charitable Choice is to the TANF block grant—funds that are provided to the states (and sometimes, in turn, to local jurisdictions). What could Congress have possibly meant by inserting subsections (b), (d)(1), and (d)(2)(A), collectively, except to have the directives of those subsections bear down on how state and local governments spent their TANF funds? That, of course, means that these subsections should be given real and meaningful preemptive effect when it comes to state or local procurement laws that undermine the religious freedom of faith-based organizations. To deny the freedom of religious staffing is one of the most certain means of secularizing a faith-based organization.[119]

Subsection (d)(1) is remedial and should be read in light of its purpose clearly stated in subsection (b), that is, to allow faith-based organizations to become program grantees "without impairing the religious character" of such providers. There is no general release for faith-based providers from following program rules. Rules to protect health, safety, and the general welfare are the subject of police power laws and not procurement regulations, so the preemption standard in subsection (d) does not even apply. As explained above, the word "retain" in subsection (d)(1) means only procurement rules are subject to preemption, not police power laws. Nor are faith-based organizations relieved of proper accounting or the duty

---

and local nondiscrimination procurement laws. See, e.g., Rep. Bobby Scott's floor argument to the effect that a bill with Charitable Choice provisions should not be enacted because Charitable Choice permits discrimination in employment by religious groups, determining who can and cannot get jobs. 146 CONG. REC. H6797, H6827□28, H6837 (July 25, 2000).

[119] The same consideration applies to Charitable Choice for CSBG and SAMHSA funds. Almost all of these federal funds are transferred to state or local governments, rather than being directly awarded by federal officials to nongovernmental organizations. So the congressional directives concerning the independence of faith-based providers are largely meant for state and local officials.

to serve all clients. To erase any doubt, Congress drafted provisions into the text of Charitable Choice to prohibit religious discrimination against welfare clients (*see* § 604a(g)), and to provide for fiscal audits (*see* § 604a(h)).

Some opponents of the faith-based initiative argue that subsection (d) should be read as preempting only laws that intentionally single-out religious charities for discrimination in grant eligibility. That makes no sense. A no-intentional-discrimination rule is already laid down in subsection (c) (§ 604a(c)). Second, the Free Exercise Clause already makes unlawful laws that intentionally discriminate against religion and religious organizations.[120] So the opponents' limiting view of subsection (d) would render the "independence" language redundant with both the Free Exercise Clause and subsection (c). Finally, the expansive terms of subsection (d) ("shall retain its independence . . . including such organization's control over the definition, development, practice, and expression of its religious beliefs") cannot fairly be read in such a crabbed manner.

Still other opponents argue that the presence in Charitable Choice of a separate subsection (f) (§ 604a(f)), dealing with Title VII of the Civil Rights Act of 1964 and employment discrimination, implies that subsection (d) does not deal with employment discrimination. In other words, they argue that to the extent Charitable Choice deals with the freedom of religious staffing, it does so in subsection (f) alone, not subsection (d). That argument is mistaken for two reasons. First, subsection (d) does not do the same work as subsection (f). Indeed, they do not even so much as overlap. Subsection (d) overturns only procurement laws, and does so only when a procurement law conflicts with a sincerely held belief that goes to the "religious character" or religious "independence" of the faith-based organization.

---

[120]*See Church of the Lukumi Babalu Aye, Inc. v. City of Hialeah*, 508 U.S. 520 (1993) (finding that municipal ordinances that intentionally discriminated against ritual sacrifice of animals violate Free Exercise Clause).

Subsection (f) is about 702(a) of Title VII, which is not a procurement law but a law based on the congressional power to regulate interstate commerce (analogous to a state police power law). In subsection (f), Congress merely sought to state the truism that when a religious organization is awarded a federal grant it does not forfeit its employment protection in 702(a).[121]

Second, in subsection (f) Congress was both pointed and emphatic in preserving 702(a) so that religious organizations would be assured that they could continue to staff on a religious basis. If, so far as Title VII goes, Congress saw fit to ensure the preservation of the freedom of religious staffing, it logically follows that Congress would seek the same freedom to staff vis-à-vis state and local procurement laws. Why bother to preserve the former freedom if Congress did not finish the job by doing the latter? Recall that almost all of the money governed by Charitable Choice is sent by the federal government to state or local authorities before it is awarded to faith-based or secular providers. Subsection (f)—rather than undermining the preemptive force of subsection (d)—actually is an added assurance that the scope of religious "independence" in subsection (d) was intended to preempt contrary state and local employment nondiscrimination procurement laws.

Finally, some opponents argue that subsection (d) means only that faith-based organizations retain their independence "outside" the government-funded program, but not "inside" the funded program. That is not logical. Procurement laws operate only "inside" a funded program, so that is where the religious provider needs its autonomy preserved—not "outside" the

---

[121] Stating such a truism was no hollow act. First, opponents of Charitable Choice have long been pointing to *Dodge v. Salvation Army*, 1989 WL 53857 (S.D. Miss. 1989), for the contrary principle of law. The *Dodge* case is shown to be in error in Chapter 2 (B)(4). Second, as previously noted, a substantial number of state and local jurisdictions do not impose a restriction on religious staffing through their own police power rules. By explicitly stating that 702(a) is preserved, Charitable Choice countered the widespread but mistaken belief that, simply by receiving federal funds, a religious organization forfeits its religious staffing freedom.

program. The whole purpose of Charitable Choice was to reassure religious charities that they could take government funds and not lose their freedom while delivering funded services. The opponents' interpretation wholly fails that basic purpose of the Charitable Choice law. Consider a parallel situation. When subsection (d)(2)(B) (§ 604a(d)(2)(B)) says a funded faith-based organization can keep up on its walls religious symbols, it does not mean the organization can keep on its walls those symbols only when providing services "outside" the funded program. Under the opponents' view, faith-based providers would daily be kept busy taking down and putting up their religious symbols as program funding switched from federal to private and back to federal. That makes no sense. By the same token, then, the autonomy language in subsection (d)(1) cannot mean that a faith-based provider retains its autonomy only "outside" the funded program.

There is one exception to the rule of Charitable Choice preemption of state and local nondiscrimination procurement laws. Charitable Choice for SAMHSA programs does not preempt such state laws, although, it does continue to preempt such local governmental laws.[122] This is the consequence of a no-preemption or "saving" provision placed by Congress in the December 2000 SAMHSA implementing legislation.[123] This compromise is instructive, however. It shows that those in Congress who opposed the preemptive effect of Charitable Choice on state and local procurement nondiscrimination laws knew that the only way to prevent such preemption was to override the "retain religious independence" clause with a "saving" provision.

---

[122]This is reflected in the HHS regulations for SAMHSA, 42 C.F.R. §§ 54.6(c), 54a.6(c).

[123]42 U.S.C. § 290kk-1(e). This statutory provision is explained at 68 Fed. Reg. 56429, 56436 (Sept. 30, 2003).

2. Federal Funds Not Subject to Charitable Choice Safeguards

In about a third of the states, and in many large cities and counties, faith-based organizations that enter into state or local social-service agreements are not expressly exempt from the prohibition in procurement laws on religious discrimination in employment.[124] When the federal social-service funds channeled through these governments are not subject to Charitable Choice, then faith-based organizations are presumptively subject to the religious staffing restriction. We say "presumptively" because faith-based organizations will surely raise their rights under the U.S. Constitution as well as under parallel provisions in many state constitutions and statutes.[125]

By way of illustration, assume that a state or local government receives monies under a federal social-service program not subject to Charitable Choice. Further assume that the state or local government attaches to these federal funds a procurement rule prohibiting employment discrimination on the basis of religion. Finally, assume that a faith-based organization has applied for a grant or contract from the state or local government which entails, at least in part, these federal funds.

If the state or local government denies the application because the faith-

---

[124]Ira C. Lupu and Robert W. Tuttle, *Government Partnerships with Faith-Based Service Providers: The State of the Law* 47-48 and Appendix B (Roundtable on Religion and Social Welfare Policy, December 2002), *available at* <http://www.religionandsocialpolicy.org/docs/legal/reports/12-4-2002_state_of_the_law.pdf>; Paul Taylor, *The Costs of Denying Religious Organizations the Right to Staff on a Religious Basis When They Join Federal Social Service Efforts*, 1 George Mason University Civil Rights Law Journal 159, 196 n.128 (2002) (collecting procurement laws from eleven states that prohibit religious discrimination).

[125]A number of states have enacted their own religious freedom restoration acts, which may be used to override state or local restrictions on religious staffing. Alabama has amended its state constitution to include RFRA provisions, while Illinois, Florida, Texas, Arizona, Connecticut, Oklahoma, Rhode Island, South Carolina, Idaho, New Mexico, New York, and Missouri have all passed RFRA statutes through their state legislatures. Ala. Const. Amend. No. 622. 775 Ill. Comp. Stat. 35; Fl. Stat. chs. 761.01-05; Tex. Civ. Prac. & Rem. §§ 110.001-012; Ariz. Rev. Stat. § 41-1493; Conn. Gen. Stat. § 52-571b; Okla. Stat. tit. 51, §§ 251-58; R.I. Gen. Laws § 42-80.1-1 et seq.; S.C. Code Ann. § 1-32-10 et seq.; Idaho Code § 73-401 et seq.; N.M. Stat. Ann. § 28-22-1 et seq.; Mo. Rev. Stat. §§ 1.302, 1.307.

based organization intends to staff on a religious basis in providing the services, then the faith-based organization will argue that the procurement rule imposes an unconstitutional condition.[126] More specifically, religious charities will argue that the procurement laws are not neutral as to religion. The nondiscrimination laws, by their very terms, single-out religious providers for burdens not borne by others. Religious staffing is the same freedom that other ideology-based organizations enjoy—be it the Sierra Club, the Libertarian Party, or Planned Parenthood—to ensure that their employees are committed to the organization's core mission. Sierra Club limits hiring to "greens," the Libertarian Party limits hiring to *laissez-faire* capitalists, and Planned Parenthood limits hiring to those who are "pro-choice." To be consistent with neutrality theory, that is, substantive equality for all these groups, faith-based organizations must be able to staff on a religious basis.[127] The failure of neutral treatment by the procurement laws will be said by religious charities to be a violation of the Free Exercise Clause.[128]

Additionally, recall that Congress amended Title VII in the Equal

---

[126]If the procurement rule also sought to regulate how the faith-based organization spent its privately raised funds, including the spending of such private funds to employ those of like-minded faith, that would be an unconstitutional condition. *See FCC v. League of Women Voters*, 468 U.S. 364 (1984) (striking down a government attempt to leverage government funds to restrict an organization's privately funded speech activity).

[127]Both the federal regulations and the White House are of the view that it is discrimination when organizations such as the World Wildlife Federation or Planned Parenthood are able to favor in hiring environmentalists or the pro-choice, but a religious group cannot favor in hiring those of like-minded faith. *See, e.g.,* Department of Justice commentary on its faith-based regulations, 69 Fed. Reg. 2832, 2836 (Jan. 21, 2004), *excerpted in* Appendix 7; White House Office of Faith-Based and Community Initiatives, Executive Office of the President, *Protecting the Civil Rights and Religious Liberty of Faith-Based Organizations: Why Religious Hiring Rights Must Be Preserved* 3 (June 23, 2003), *available at* <http://www.white house.gov/government/fbci/booklet.pdf>, and *reprinted in* Appendix 8.

[128]Such a free exercise claim is not blocked by *Oregon Employment Div. v. Smith*, 494 U.S. 872 (1990). In *Smith*, the Supreme Court held that there is no cause of action under the Free Exercise Clause when the law complained of is neutral as to religion and generally applicable. An employment nondiscrimination procurement law that by its terms prohibits discrimination on the basis of religion is not neutral as to religion. To claim that the law is neutral because the Sierra Club or Planned Parenthood also must not discriminate on the basis of religion makes no sense. It is like the claim that a law criminalizing the homeless sleeping under bridges is neutral because the law is equally enforced against both the rich and the poor.

Opportunity Act of 1972, in order to expand the religious staffing freedom acknowledged in 702. Congress did so, as discussed in Chapter 2, in order to keep government from unconstitutionally interfering with religious organizations. The matter of concern was church autonomy, and hence, non-entanglement or church-state separation. Traditionally, this is the concern of the Establishment Clause which faith-based organizations will argue is violated by these restrictive state and local procurement laws.[129]

Moreover, faith-based organizations will argue that the denial of funding is an unconstitutional burden on the organization's freedom of association. An ideologically driven noncommercial organization has the right to define who will constitute the group of people that formulates its vision, to determine the employees who will express that core message on behalf of the group, and to exercise the ability to exclude competing messages from being intermingled with that of the group.

Finally, faith-based organizations will argue that the denial of funding is a form of viewpoint or content-based discrimination in the distribution of a public benefit, in violation of the organization's freedom of speech. The organization's message is intertwined with its social-service mission, for that is what it means to be an ideologically driven organization. The grant would not have been denied but for the faith-based organization's expressional practice of employing those of like-minded faith to conduct its charitable calling or mission.

There is decisional law under the First Amendment supportive of these claims.[130] The state or local government can be expected to raise counter

---

[129] *See* Carl H. Esbeck, *The Establishment Clause as a Structural Restraint on Governmental Power*, 1 Iowa Law Review 1-113 (1998). The limitations set forth in *Oregon Employment Div. v. Smith*, 494 U.S. 872 (1990), to the extent relevant here, pertain only to the Free Exercise Clause and not the Establishment Clause.

[130] *See, e.g., Legal Services Corporation v. Velazquez*, 531 U.S. 533 (2001) (invalidating expressional restriction on government-funded legal services to the poor); *Boy Scouts of America v. Dale*, 530 U.S. 640 (2000) (finding that it was denial of freedom of association for a state to impose nondiscrimination requirement in the selection of adult leaders of character-building organization for youth); *Hurley v.*

arguments. It will likely rely on decisions that have permitted the placing of conditions on programs that the government subsidizes.[131] The law of unconstitutional conditions often comes down to semantics, that is, whether the courts envision the condition as a "penalty" or as merely a decision not to "include" the claimant's desired activity within the description of the funded social-service program. Here, the federal government is purchasing social services, services which faith-based providers are ready and competent to provide. For a state or local government to exclude them from the competition for program grants merely because they exercise the freedom of religious staffing certainly appears to be wholly unrelated to the purpose of the federal program. After all, the program is not a jobs program. And the program is of federal design, not a state creation. Because the state or local condition is not "germane" to the federal program design, it certainly has all the appearance of a "penalty" on First Amendment freedom, as opposed to merely the relevant manner by which the government sought to describe the targeted need of the social-service program in question.

The foregoing First Amendment rights of faith-based organizations have been greatly bolstered by federal regulations issued pursuant to Executive Order 13279 (Dec. 12, 2002).[132] The Executive Order directed

---

Irish-Am. Gay, Lesbian & Bisexual Group, 515 U.S. 557 (1995) (striking down application of state civil rights discrimination law to compel private organization to admit to its public parade a unit with a message that the organization did not want to endorse); *Peter v. Wedl*, 155 F.3d 992, 996 (8th Cir. 1998) (affirming ruling that both Free Exercise Clause and Free Speech Clause are violated by Minnesota regulations that provided aid to special education students except when the student was enrolled in a religious school; the regulation was purposefully discriminatory on the basis of religion and not required by the Establishment Clause); *Hartman v. Stone*, 68 F.3d 973 (6th Cir. 1995) (striking down, as violative of the Free Exercise Clause, U.S. Army regulation that extended benefits to private daycare centers, but not private religious daycare centers).

[131] *See Locke v. Davey*, 540 U.S., 124 S.Ct. 1307 (2004) (upholding, as consistent with Free Exercise Clause, a state's longstanding condition in its constitution on merit-based scholarships not being utilized by students to seek a higher education degree that leads to religious clerical or ministerial vocation).

[132] The Executive Order entitled "Equal Protection of the Laws for Faith-Based and Community Organizations and Permitting Religious Staffing by Faith-Based Federal Contractors," was signed on December 12, 2002, and published in the Federal Register on December 16, 2002. *See* 67 Fed. Reg. 77141. It is reprinted in Appendix 6.

each federal department administering a social-service program to thoroughly review its policies and regulations. Among other things, the review was to be with an eye to each department ensuring that: (1) social-service providers not be discriminated against on account of their religious character; and (2) social-service providers be able to participate while "retaining their independence from government and retaining control over the definition, development, practice, and expression of their religious belief."[133]

Executive Order 13279 goes on to expressly address the matter of religious staffing by amending the decades-old Executive Order 11246.[134] The amendment allows religious charities contracting with the federal government to provide social services and to offer goods and services to federal agencies, all while staffing on a religious basis.

The regulations promulgated by the federal departments pursuant to Executive Order 13279, beginning in mid-2003, have set out the twin aims of equal treatment of all providers without regard to religion and the retention of a faith-based organization's religious autonomy.[135] Although the recent regulations do not expressly state that they preempt state and local employment nondiscrimination procurement laws, in inescapable

---

[133]These two requirements, which also appear in the rules for Charitable Choice, were immediately objected to by opponents of the faith-based initiative as protecting religious staffing rights. *See, e.g., American Jewish Committee Alarmed at President Bush's Charitable Choice Order,* AJC Press Release of Dec. 12, 2002, *available at* <http://www.ajc.org/InTheMedia/PressReleases.asp?did=707>; *Anti-Defamation League Urges President Bush to Reconsider Executive Order on Faith-Based Initiatives,* ADL Press Release of Dec. 12, 2002, *available at* <http://www.adl.org/PresRele/ RelChStSep_90/4210_32.htm>.

[134]*See* Executive Order 13279, 67 Fed. Reg. 77143 § 4. As discussed in Chapter 2, E.O. 11246 covers federal contracts, not federal grants and cooperative agreements.

[135]See Appendix 2 for a listing of regulations that have been promulgated or proposed to implement the equal treatment principles of the Executive Order. The Department of Justice equal treatment final rule is excerpted in Appendix 7. These various equal treatment regulations apply to programs other than those covered by Charitable Choice provisions, apply whether the federal funds are administered by federal, state, or local officials, and apply to any state or local funds that are commingled with the federal funds or that are required by law to be matched with them.

ways the regulations, applied straightforwardly, conflict with and thus do override these restrictive procurement laws.[136] That is, if an organization is to have an equal opportunity to compete for a grant without regard to religion and the organization is to retain its independence from state and local governments, then such an organization's religious staffing freedom inescapably follows. The regulatory comments not only give notice that federal funds carry federal requirements, but the overall thrust of the federal regulatory effort is in obvious appreciation that the faith-based initiative includes the staffing freedom. This is further evident by the explicit amending of Executive Order 11246 to allow for religious staffing in contracts, the explicit preserving of 702(a) of Title VII to allow for religious staffing,[137] and the explicit acknowledging of RFRA's applicability to federal laws that burden religious exercise.[138]

The legal force of each department's regulation follows the federal funds, so that when those funds are passed on to state and local governments, the regulations are far-reaching in their impact on state and local laws. The regulations under Executive Order 13279 not only apply to grants awarded directly by federal agencies, but also to federal monies sent to state and local governments and later awarded by them, as well as to any matching funds those governments must provide, and to funds a state or

---

[136]See, for example, the regulations issued by the Department of Justice. 28 C.F.R. § 38.2 pertains to formula grants, that is, monies initially provided to state and local governments. Sec. 38.2(a) requires that faith-based organizations not be discriminated against. That means if Sierra Club can hire only environmentalists, faith-based organizations can hire only those of like-minded faith. Sec. 38.2(c) says that these organizations retain their religious autonomy, including "authority over their internal governance." Sec. 38.2(e) says that state and local governments cannot promulgate rules that disqualify faith-based organizations on the grounds that "such organizations are motivated or influenced by religious faith to provide social services, or because of their religious character or affiliation." The final rule is excerpted in Appendix 7. A straightforward application of these regulatory safeguards would mean that religious staffing is protected.

[137]See, e.g., 28 C.F.R. § 38.2(f).

[138]See, for example, the Department of Justice comment on the applicability of RFRA, 69 Fed. Reg. 2832, 2836 (Jan. 21, 2004) (the final rule is excerpted in Appendix 7), and the similar Department of Health and Human Services comment, 69 Fed. Reg. 42591 (July 16, 2004).

locality voluntarily adds to, and commingles with, the federal funds.[139]

If a state or local agency fails to permit religious staffing by a religious charity, the charity may notify the appropriate federal agency. The agency, of course, has the authority, indeed, the duty, to investigate and, if need be, to enforce its regulations and the intent of Executive Order 13279. Charitable Choice in TANF does expressly provide a private cause of action to religious charities.[140]

Just how these conflicting claims will be resolved is presently unknown. Congress may act to clarify its use of federal spending power, and the Executive Branch could do more by way of additional clarifying regulations and internal policies. Such actions would be helpful. However, as things now stand, further litigation may follow to ultimately answer all of these conflicting perspectives on the religious freedom and equal-treatment demands of the First Amendment, as well as on the scope of the Executive Branch's regulatory authority.[141]

It is wrong to shift this burden of uncertainty, as well as the risk and expense of litigation, to religious charities. Congress should act to remove any remaining doubt concerning religious staffing rights taking precedent over state and local restrictive procurement rules. There is something to be said for federalism in many circumstances, but here the monies are originally federal funds rather than tax funds raised by the states, and the programs are of federal design and purpose. Federal funds should be subject

---

[139]Federal monies provided to states and to local governments may require the addition of matching funds or sometimes "maintenance of effort" funds. These required funds are subject to the federal rules. Thus, wherever there are federal funds, in whole or in part, the federal regulations must be followed rather than conflicting state or local procurement laws.

[140]In 42 U.S.C. § 604a(i), Charitable Choice provides for a private right of action for injunctive relief. The provisions are reprinted in Appendix 3.

[141]See Fidelity Fed'l Savings & Loan Assoc. v. De La Cuesta, 458 U.S. 141, 152-53 (1982) (finding preemption by operation of federal regulation); Geier v. American Honda Motor Co., 529 U.S. 861, 869-74 (2000) (finding conflict preemption and that a save-from-preemption clause was inapplicable).

to the federal program rules, notwithstanding conflicting state or local rules, and regardless of the state, county, or city where the federal program operates. Nationwide legal uniformity will hasten social-services reform, and the greater simplicity for grant applicants that comes with uniformity will increase provider efficiency and save the government money. The continued threat of restrictive procurement rules in some state and municipal jurisdictions only operates to keep religious providers from expanding their works of compassion. The continued uncertainty hurts the poor and needy.

5   *Religious Staffing: The Policy Justifications*

When proponents of the faith-based initiative advocate for religious staffing by faith-based organizations that collaborate with government to address social needs, they are not seeking to "roll back decades of civil rights advances," as some critics have asserted. Rather, they are seeking to clarify and secure the civil rights of faith-based organizations and thereby help the poor. As the White House statement on religious staffing says:

> For nearly forty years, the Civil Rights Act of 1964 has respected the right of religious groups to make religiously based employment decisions . . . . Some laws protect the hiring rights of faith-based groups that receive Federal funds, and others do not . . . . [T]his tangle of laws has discouraged many effective faith-based providers from competing to provide government-funded services. The real victims of this contradictory statutory scheme are, of course, the needy Americans who could be helped by faith-based providers.[142]

---

[142]White House Office of Faith-Based and Community Initiatives, *Protecting the Civil Rights and Religious Liberty of Faith-Based Organizations: Why Religious Hiring Rights Must Be Preserved* 1, 7 (June 23, 2003), *available at* <http://www.whitehouse.gov/government/fbci/booklet.pdf>, *reprinted in* Appendix 8.

In an era in which government plays such a huge role in funding social services, the promise of the 1964 Civil Rights Act to secure the religious staffing freedom can best be fulfilled by having Congress act to ensure that religious providers not lose that freedom when they accept government money.

> Faith-based organizations must be protected from the kind of discrimination that would prevent us from hiring the people who are best equipped to fulfill our mission and do the work, work that has been proven to be effective time and again. This discrimination is a violation of the civil rights of religious groups and would effectively prevent the delivery of services to this country's black and brown urban poor.
>
> —Rev. Eugene F. Rivers, III, National Ten Point Leadership Foundation, Boston
> (quoted in *White House Office of Faith-Based and Community Initiatives,*
> *Protecting the Civil Rights and Religious Liberty of Faith-Based*
> *Organizations: Why Religious Hiring Rights Must be Preserved* (2003)).

A. A faith-based organization's decision to employ staff who share its religious beliefs is not an act of shameful intolerance but a laudable and positive act of freedom.

In a pluralistic society that properly honors the freedom of association, a wide variety of ideology-based organizations rightly are at liberty to select employees who share their core commitments. Environmental organizations, feminist groups, unions, and political parties are all free to choose staff who subscribe to their central ideology. This freedom should not disappear when a government invites these private-sector organizations to collaborate with it to perform some public task. Planned Parenthood, for example, does not and should not lose its freedom to hire pro-choice staff simply because it has a government contract. To deny this same freedom to religious organizations is discriminatory and not a fit policy for a society in which all are equal before the law.

It is confusion to equate this positive good with the evil of discrimination on the basis of race or sex. Our opponents would lump together religious discrimination with, say, discrimination on the basis of race or ethnicity. Disapproving of a job applicant because of his or her race is indeed senseless and often malicious. But one's religious beliefs speak real and important differences about the nature of life, which in turn shape one's vocational purpose and job performance. One who has never disagreed with others about religion is not an open-minded tolerant individual, but is treating religion as trivial as if religious beliefs do not matter. To regard religious differences to be of no serious consequence, as mere personal preferences or cultural habits, is to denigrate religion. This is actually a form of bigotry under the guise of "religious tolerance." Behind this thinking is that religion does not mean anything or ought not to be taken seriously, and so is fair game for attack the moment religious people actually assert its meaningfulness in, for example, employment practices about hiring those of like-minded faith. What is called for here is true religious pluralism, not a *pseudo* tolerance where religion is considered to be as unimportant as whether one drives a Ford or a Chevy. Genuine religious pluralism, to which our First Amendment is dedicated, is where Catholics are allowed to be Catholics, Jews are Jews, and evangelical Protestants act as evangelicals. Freedom is operative when every religious organization is permitted to live within its fundamental value system, with equality and tolerance by the government.[143]

As pointed out by Nathan Diament of the Union of Orthodox Jewish Congregations of America, in today's America, religious groups reflect society's demographic diversity. "There are now black Jews, Asian Evangelicals, white Muslims, and these trends will only increase. This is because, at their core, religious groups don't care about where you come from or what you look like, only what you believe."[144] Whether one thinks that religion is a backward superstition that modern, rational folk ought to abandon or an inherent trait of humanity that generally contributes to

---

[143] *See* Stephen L. Carter, *The Culture of Disbelief: How American Law and Politics Trivialize Religious Devotion* (1993).

[144] Nathan J. Diament, *A Slander Against Our Sacred Institutions*, Washington Post, May 28, 2001, at A23.

societal well-being, all who believe in freedom of expressive association for cause-oriented groups should insist that the religious staffing freedom for faith-based organizations is something positive to be protected by law rather than an evil to be scorned and suppressed.

B. The ability to choose staff who share a religious organization's beliefs is essential to that organization's retention of its core identity.

As noted in Chapter 2, U.S. Supreme Court Justice William Brennan in *Corporation of the Presiding Bishop v. Amos* observed that determining whether "certain activities are in furtherance of an organization's religious mission and that only those committed to that mission should conduct them, is . . . a means by which a religious community defines itself."[145] Having employees who share a faith-based organization's religious beliefs profoundly shapes the organization's character in a variety of ways. Similar values, a sense of community, unity of purpose, and shared experiences of prayer and worship as colleagues all contribute to an *esprit de corps* and common vision.[146] As law professor Ira C. Lupu says, "the sense of religious community and spirit on which success of the group's efforts depend" may be hampered if faith-based organizations are forced to hire those who do not share an organization's beliefs.[147]

> [I]t's obvious, on reflection, that without the ability to discriminate on the basis of religion in hiring and firing staff, religious organizations lose the right to define their organizational mission enjoyed by secular organizations that receive public funds.
> —Jeffrey Rosen, *Religious Rights: Why the Catholic Church Shouldn't Have to Hire Gays*, The New Republic, Feb. 26, 2001.

---

[145] *Amos*, 483 U.S. 327, 342 (1987).

[146] *See* Jeffrey Rosen, *Religious Rights: Why the Catholic Church Shouldn't Have to Hire Gays*, The New Republic, Feb. 26, 2001, at 16-17.

[147] *The Constitutional Role Of Faith-Based Organizations in Competitions for Federal Social Service Funds*, Testimony by Ira C. Lupu; before the House Subcomm. on the Constitution, Comm. On the

Religious staffing is essential even though faith-based organizations with government grants keep worship, religious instruction, and evangelism separate from the government-funded social services. This is so for multiple reasons. First, by experience these organizations have learned that religion is important to the overall success of a social service even though religious activities are voluntary, privately funded, and separate from the government-funded program. In such organizations, religious faith and practice are no less important qualifications for a staff position than are technical skills or educational degrees.

Second, if a faith-based organization is forced to accept staff without regard to religious commitment, then religious expression within the organization is likely to be stifled. Employees will fear offending other employees who do not believe or who belong to other faiths. Since personal faith is often important to those who choose to work in a religious organization, such an uncertain climate will diminish staff motivation and effectiveness. Indeed, it may lead to lawsuits by employees outside the organization's faith community bringing claims of a hostile work environment or religious harassment.[148] Forced religious heterogeneity will sap an organization's spiritual vitality and send it down the path of secularization.

Third, it is common for staff to hold multiple jobs, especially in small organizations or those with tight budgets. For example, a small faith-based organization might seek someone to be a half-time youth minister and a half-time social worker in its youth mentoring program. Permitting the organization to hire on a religious basis for some jobs but not for others will lead to complicated and entangling regulation.

Judiciary, 107th Cong., 1st Sess., 18 (June 7, 2001), *available at* <http://www/house.gov/judiciary/lupu_060701>.

[148]*See* Michael Wolf, et al., *Religion in the Workplace: A Comprehensive Guide To Legal Rights and Responsibilities* 55-66,157-162 (1998).

C. The religious staffing freedom undergirds, rather than undermines, a diverse and pluralistic society.

Opponents of religious staffing by faith-based organizations sometimes claim the high ground of promoting diversity. Our nation is pluralistic and values diversity, they point out. So it is legitimate, they argue, for government to promote and protect diversity by requiring organizations— particularly those it helps fund—to accept staff without regard to race, color, ethnicity, sex, age, disability . . . or religion.

Yet forcing faith-based organizations to hire without regard to religion is, in truth, a sure recipe for a less diverse society. It is not possible for a religious organization of a particular faith to retain the characteristics and tenets of that faith, if it is forbidden to take religion into account in its employment decisions. A Lutheran foster-care home would soon be Lutheran in name only if it had to hire people of any faith, and no faith, throughout the organization. Likewise with regard to a Jewish day school, an evangelical Protestant housing rehab organization, or a Catholic community development program. There can be little enduring societal diversity among religious social-service providers if every faith-based organization is forced to incorporate religious diversity within itself. Additionally, the religious diversity of the larger civil society will be flattened out if religious staffing is outlawed, just as political organizations would be able to offer the public few real choices if political parties were forced to employ staff without regard to political belief.

> Jewish and non-Jewish opponents of President Bush's faith-based initiative have emphasized the possibility that, under the president's program, Christian institutions will refuse to hire Jews even though they accept tax funds. It is undoubtedly true that some will do so. There is already litigation in at least one such case and that challenge is endorsed by leaders of the local Jewish federation. The federation is apparently oblivious to the fact that it, and many, if not all, of its beneficiaries practice exactly the same discrimination. Indeed, they would not be recognizably Jewish if they did not.
>
> --Marc Stern (American Jewish Congress),
> *Cracks Form in the Wall of Separation*, Forward, Nov. 14, 2003.

D. Just because a private-sector organization, including one that is faith-based, accepts some federal funds, it does not cease to exist as a separate entity and become a mere arm of the government.

Some have argued that private associations must give up private associational rights when they accept government support, because they become, in part, de facto public entities. This makes no sense, for the argument assumes a dependent status for nongovernmental organizations that makes impossible a free and open society.

Both case law and common sense argue that a private-sector organization that receives government funds still retains its separate identity.[149] Were this not so, the government—due to heavy spending of tax dollars—will have swallowed up a large part of the private sector. But, in fact, there are many nongovernmental organizations: private groups, organizations of the "third sector," the "independent sector," or the "voluntary sector." A division between public and private is universally acknowledged in such instances as colleges and universities receiving government funding, scholars engaging in federally subsidized research, and artists and artistic organizations being supported by the National Endowment for the Arts.

All of these receive government funding. All maintain their autonomy and liberty of expression. All maintain their academic and artistic freedom. They are not, even in part, arms of the government. Similarly, a faith-based organization that receives government funds to provide a social service that the legislature has decided is for the common good must be free to maintain its independent character and autonomy. Among other things, this means a faith-based organization must retain its right to use religious criteria in making employment decisions.

---

[149] The Supreme Court cases rejecting the argument that the receipt of government funding by a private organization renders that organization a "state actor" or "federal actor" and thus subject to the Establishment Clause are discussed in Chapter 2 (B)(2).

E. Permitting faith-based organizations that receive social-service grants the freedom to staff on a religious basis is the only way to avoid viewpoint discrimination by the government.

Vast sums of government money flow to many different types of private-sector social-service providers. Some of these providers engage in inherently religious activities separate from the government-funded program, others do not. Some religious charities take religion into account for all staff positions while others are concerned with the religious convictions only of governing-level staff. Still other providers, while animated by a major cause, do not understand that cause in religious terms and are thus regarded as "secular" providers.

Religious organizations are purposive, committed to substantive ends and not merely procedural fairness. Intentionally religious or faith-centered organizations hire employees who share their beliefs. They do so precisely because of their religious conviction that persons (both staff and beneficiaries) are spiritual as well as material beings, and therefore the best results follow when spiritual and material transformation are both operative. Other organizations, termed church-related or faith-affiliated, sometimes ignore religion in staffing decisions because their religious worldview holds that social problems and destructive social behavior can be corrected by socio-economic change, thus putting religion to the side. A third group, secular providers, implicitly or explicitly have adopted a naturalistic perspective that denies the existence of a spiritual or religious dimension. All three types of providers—faith-centered, religiously affiliated, and secular[150]—operate on the basis of a worldview, a set of deep convictions, a religious or ideological perspective.

If the government's program or procurement laws mean that only

---

[150]For further discussion of these categories, see Ronald J. Sider and Heidi Rolland Unruh, *Typology of Religious Characteristics of Social Service and Educational Organizations and Programs*, Nonprofit and Voluntary Sector Quarterly 109-134 (March 2004).

independent-sector providers willing to ignore religion in staffing decisions can be funded, then, intentionally or not, the government is discriminating among competing faiths or worldviews, privileging those whose deepest conviction is that religion is irrelevant in employment decisions. Such discrimination favors those providers with views that are currently "politically correct" because they are not, for example, explicitly Jewish or "Protestant fundamentalist" or "proselytizing." It subordinates the robustly religious to the equally ideological, but "secular," worldview. By marginalizing overtly faith-based services, it narrows the range of choices available to the needy, some of whom would like the choice to receive services at faith-centered providers.

F. Prohibiting government funding for faith-based social-service providers that staff on a religious basis will hurt the poor and needy.

In a July, 2001, *Wall Street Journal* op-ed, Andrew Young asked, "Why should the (faith-based) organizations that are best at serving the needy be excluded from even applying for government funding?"[151] Urging Senate passage of legislation that would expand Charitable Choice to additional federal social programs, Young warned opponents against playing politics with the poor and needy.

Young's premise, of course, may be mistaken. He assumes that many of the poor need moral and spiritual change as well as material transformation, and that faith-based organizations are often more effective than secular providers. There are no extensive comparative quantitative studies demonstrating that intensely faith-centered social-service providers produce better results, nor is it likely that faith-based providers will always be

---

[151] Andrew Young, *Are Democrats Putting Politics Over the Needy?*, Wall Street Journal, July 23, 2001, at A 4.

better—or worse—than secular programs. There is considerable anecdotal data, however, suggesting that thoroughly faith-centered programs are producing remarkable outcomes where almost nothing else seems to work—such as in assisting the drug-addicted, the welfare-dependent, the recidivist, and the persistently homeless.[152]

Such a finding fits well with the vast number of quantitative studies demonstrating that for many people religion contributes positively to emotional and physical well being.[153] The success stories often come from religious organizations, or from those they have helped—both of whom are certain that the faith-factor in the program is a cause of their success. If they are right, then refusing to fund such organizations means denying many of our most needy citizens the best available help.

G. Because government is now asking religious groups to provide more social services, it should reciprocate by respecting the integrity of these organizations.

Religious organizations have been caring for the poor and needy for millennia. They will continue to do so, regardless of what government says or funds. Today, however, the government is asking faith-based groups to provide more social services and offering support to expand their service capacity. In part this is because of the many testimonials to the effectiveness of faith-based services and in part because religious organizations are frequently the only institutions still functioning in distressed neighborhoods. If government wants additional help, it dare not add conditions that will drive off the organizations it most hopes to attract or that will undermine the very qualities that makes those organizations

---

[152]*See, e.g.*, Stephen V. Monsma, *Putting Faith in Partnerships: Welfare-to-Work in Four Cities* (2004); Ram Cnaan, *Keeping Faith in the City* (Center for Research on Religion and Urban Civil Society, 2001).

[153]Byron Johnson, *Objective Hope: Assessing the Effectiveness of Faith-based Organizations: A Review of the Literature* (2002), *available at* <http://www.manhattan-institute.org/crrucs_objective_hope.pdf>.

uniquely effective. Honoring the freedom to staff with individuals who share the faith-based organization's beliefs is the single most important way to ensure that religious providers can deliver on the government's call for effective and expanded assistance to the needy.

H. Religious charities that staff on a religious basis are not trying to foist their religion on others, but ask only that others not impose alien values on them.

Religious charities that select staff who share their religious beliefs accept that other organizations should have the same freedom to staff based on that group's worldview or ideology. Faith-based organizations are not foisting their religious beliefs or morality upon others. Rather than imposing their own worldview on unwilling others, they simply want each cause-based organization to be free to make employment choices based on its deepest commitments. It is those seeking to deny religious staffing to religious groups who are trying to use the coercive power of the state to foist their ideological beliefs on others.

I. Denying the freedom of faith-based organizations to hire staff on the basis of religion would require drastic and widespread changes in current practice.

Religious colleges and universities, religious hospitals, religious retirement and nursing homes, religious foster-care homes and day-care centers, religious refugee-resettlement programs and overseas-development agencies, and many other religious organizations receive government funding to support their educational, health care, social-service, or development activities.[154] Many of these organizations consider the existing

---

[154]There are no firm statistics, either in general or by type of social service, of the amount of government funding that supports services provided by faith-based organizations. However, studies that include some discussion of the topic include: Stephen V. Monsma, *When Sacred and Secular Mix: Religious Nonprofit Organizations and Public Money* (1996); J. Bruce Nichols, *The Uneasy Alliance:*

and long-recognized staffing freedom to be essential to their effective provision of services. Those who oppose religious staffing in the context of Charitable Choice or the faith-based initiative, if they are consistent, must seek to overturn and outlaw this vast range of collaborations in which the government currently supports faith-based organizations.

> To maintain its very identity, a religious or faith-based organization must be able to consider an individual's religious affiliation and willingness to support the mission and values of the institution when making employment decisions. Congress recognized this need when it passed the Civil Rights Act of 1964, by specifically exempting religious employers from the Title VII restrictions on consideration of religion in hiring decisions, and again in 1972 when it clarified the reach of the exemption.
>
> —*Joint letter to Congress* by Cardinal Theodore McCarrick, Chairman of the Domestic Policy Committee, U.S. Conference of Catholic Bishops; Thomas A. DeStefano, President of Catholic Charities USA; and Rev. Michael D. Place, President and Chief Executive Officer of the Catholic Health Association USA, concerning bill HR 3030, Improving the Community Services Block Grant Act (2004).

Such a radical disruption of existing higher educational services and the government-supported social safety net would be tragic. It would harm not only the faith-based organizations but the millions of people and thousands of neighborhoods that count on their services. And such a change is entirely unnecessary. Civil rights and religious freedom need not, and should not, be pitted against each other. Faith-based organizations, whether they find their support entirely from private sources or accept some government funding, should be free to select the staff most compatible with and dedicated to their faith-based mission of helping the needy. Such a policy does not contradict civil rights but expands it.

Religion, Refugee Work, and U.S. Foreign Policy (1988); *Who Will Provide? The Changing Role of Religion in American Social Welfare* (Mary Jo Bane et al. eds., 2000); *Sacred Places, Civic Purposes: Should Government Help Faith-Based Charity?* (E. J. Dionne, Jr. and Ming Hsu Chen eds., 2001); and Stephen V. Monsma, *Putting Faith in Partnerships: Welfare-to-Work in Four Cities* (2004).

6 *Recommendations and Precautions*

Because the freedom of faith-based organizations to staff on a religious basis is vital to many religious charities, and yet is poorly understood and honored in varying degrees by different laws, we make the following recommendations to faith-based organizations and to government officials:

A. For Faith-Based Organizations

- The point of the freedom to take faith into account in employment decisions is to be able to maintain an environment, and to provide services, that reflect your organization's deepest faith commitments. Use the freedom to enable your organization to provide the most effective help possible.

- A religiously based employment decision may appear to be capricious discrimination unless your organization has a well-developed employment policy. The board and staff should carefully work through what the organization's beliefs entail for employment, and develop a written statement of principles and standards. The policy and rationale should be clearly conveyed both to current staff and to applicants, and it must be consistently applied in practice.

- The freedom to staff on a religious basis does not release your faith-based organization from the requirement not to discriminate in employment on other grounds, such as race, color, national origin, age, disabilities, and sex, and it does not justify religious discrimination in serving the needy. Make sure that your governing board, staff, and volunteers understand when differential treatment based on religion is acceptable and even necessary, and when it is legally and morally wrong.

- If your organization has a sincerely held religious belief about certain types of employee conduct, such as sexual activity outside of marriage, it can maintain these employment standards but only if it applies them consistently, not arbitrarily. Consult with a lawyer to be sure you have appropriate written policies and have instituted appropriate practices.

- If your faith-based organization staffs on a religious basis, you will have to look carefully at the attached "strings" if you decide to consider government funding. Whether religious staffing is permitted or not depends on the specific program, the level of government, and the jurisdiction where your organization operates. You should not just presume that religious staffing is permitted, or, for that matter, forbidden. If you are unsure of the requirements after looking at the funding announcement, request for proposal, or grant agreement, consult with a lawyer.

- Because many current pronouncements about religious staffing have been misleading, and new religion-neutral rules have not been fully implemented, you should not assume that government officials and official announcements will always provide accurate information about the requirements of a particular funding program. If you suspect that your freedom is greater than officials or documents acknowledge, ask what their legal justification is for any restrictions. If necessary, consult with a lawyer, not only to find out for sure what the applicable rules are but also so that you will have leverage if it is the official, and not the law, that insists on restricting religious staffing.

- Laws and regulations that unnecessarily restrict religious freedom are unconstitutional. If officials insist that your faith-based organization has to stop considering religion in its employment decisions as the price of receiving government funds, consider challenging the restriction. Going to court or threatening legal action might be regarded as a diversion from serving the needy. However, it may also be a way to serve other faith-based organizations and, ultimately, the poor and distressed, who deserve the best help and should not be kept from choosing organizations whose faith is reflected in staff, programs, and environment.

B. For Government Officials

- Despite the loud claims of opponents of the faith-based initiative, there is no general federal statute or constitutional rule that forbids faith-based organizations that accept government funds from taking religion into account in their employment decisions. Under federal law, and often under state and local laws, faith-based organizations may staff on a religious basis, and they do not lose that freedom when they accept government funds. Do not presume the loss of the religious staffing freedom unless you know of a specific legal requirement to that effect.

- Some state and local governments have been slow to acknowledge that Congress intended faith-based organizations to be able to retain their religious staffing rights when accepting federal funds that are covered by Charitable Choice. If you administer state or local contracts or grants using these federal funds, you are obligated to make legal or administrative changes so that you can honor this intent. A faith-based organization seeking government funds may have, despite contrary laws or regulations, a legitimate claim to religious staffing due to the Constitution, the Religious Freedom Restoration Act (at the federal level), or the preemption requirements of Charitable Choice (at the state and local level). Do not reject such a claim out of hand, but instead work with the faith-based organization and with your agency's legal counsel to accommodate religious freedom.

- Employment discrimination is an evil that our society has not yet fully overcome. Religious staffing by faith-based organizations, on the other hand, is an expression of religious freedom and not a bigoted effort to limit people's employment. It is a means by which many faith-based organizations seek to maintain their religious character, just as political or ideological organizations maintain their character by hiring only like-minded employees. Faith-based organizations that insist on religious staffing are not being intolerant. Remember that they desire only to preserve their ability to serve the needy in their own distinctive way.

Appendix 1.

Selected Resources

Bibliography

David M. Ackerman, *Public Aid to Faith-Based Organizations (Charitable Choice) in the 107th Congress: Background and Selected Legal Issues*, Congressional Research Service Report for Congress, order code RL31043 (Aug. 19, 2003).

John D. Ashcroft, Statement on Charitable Choice, Proceedings and Debates of the 105th Cong. 2d Sess., 144 CONG. REC., S12686 - S12688 (Oct. 20, 1998) (Senator Ashcroft comments on the interpretation and constitutionality of Charitable Choice provisions, relative to the recent reauthorization of the Community Services Block Grant Act).

Stanley W. Carlson-Thies, *Charitable Choice: Bringing Religion Back into American Welfare in* RELIGION RETURNS TO THE PUBLIC SQUARE: FAITH AND POLICY IN AMERICA 269-97 (Hugh Heclo and Wilfred M. McClay, eds., 2003).

Stanley W. Carlson-Thies, *Charitable Choice for Welfare and Community Services: An Implementation Guide for State, Local, and Federal Officials* (2000), *available at* <http://www.cpjustice.org/charitable choice/publications>.

Stanley W. Carlson-Thies and Carl H. Esbeck, *A Guide to Charitable Choice: The Rules of Section 104 of the 1996 Federal Welfare Law Governing State Cooperation with Faith-based Social Service Providers* (1997), *available at* <http://www.cpjustice.org/ charitablechoice/guide/>.

Nathan Diament, Op-Ed, *A Slander Against Our Sacred Institutions*, Washington Post, May 28, 2001, at A23.

Dave Donaldson and Stanley W. Carlson-Thies, *A Revolution of Compassion: Faith-Based Groups as Full Partners in Fighting America's Social Problems* (2003).

Carl H. Esbeck, Statement Before the United States House of Representatives Concerning Charitable Choice and the Community Solutions Act, Subcommittee on the Constitution of the House Judiciary Committee (June 12, 2001), *reprinted at* 16 Notre Dame Journal of Law, Ethics & Public Policy 567 (2002).

Carl H. Esbeck, *The Neutral Treatment of Religion and Faith-Based Social Service Providers: Charitable Choice and Its Critics in* WELFARE REFORM AND FAITH-BASED ORGANIZATIONS 173-217 (Derek Davis and Barry Hankins, eds., 1999)

Carl H. Esbeck, *The Establishment Clause as a Structural Restraint on Governmental Power*, 84 Iowa Law Review 1-113 (1998).

Carl H. Esbeck, A *Constitutional Case for Governmental Cooperation with Faith-Based Social Service Providers*, 46 Emory Law Journal 1-42 (1997).

Carl H. Esbeck, *Equal Treatment: Its Constitutional Status in* EQUAL TREATMENT OF RELIGION IN A PLURALISTIC SOCIETY 9-29 (Stephen V. Monsma and J. Christopher Soper, eds., 1998).

Carl H. Esbeck, *The Regulation of Religious Organizations As Recipients of Governmental Assistance* (1996).

Executive Order 13199, 66 Fed. Reg. 8499 (Jan. 31, 2001) (the Executive Order created the Office of Faith-Based and Community Initiatives in the Executive Office of the President).

Executive Order 13279, 67 Fed. Reg. 77141 (Dec. 16, 2002) (the Executive Order sets out how the executive branch will ensure "equal protection of the laws for faith-based and community organizations" and amended Executive Order 11246 so that all faith-based organizations that contract with the federal government do not thereby lose their ability to staff on a religious basis).

Charles L. Glenn, *The Ambiguous Embrace: Government and Faith-Based Schools and Social Agencies,* 193-211, 291-92 (2000).

John C. Green and Amy L. Sherman, *Fruitful Collaborations: A Survey of Government-Funded Faith-Based Programs in 15 States* (Hudson Institute, September 2002), *available at* <www.hudson faithincommunities.org>.

House Committee on the Judiciary, Community Solutions Act of 2001, H.R. 7, REP. NO. 107-138, 107TH Cong., 1ST Sess. (July 12, 2001) (reporting on committee substitute for H.R. 7, together with dissenting views, which later passed the House).

Byron R. Johnson, *Objective Hope: Assessing the Effectiveness of Faith-Based Organizations: A Review of the Literature* (Center for Research on Religion and Urban Civil Society at Univ. of Penn., 2002).

Douglas Laycock, *The Constitutional Role of Faith-Based Organizations in Competitions for Federal Social Service Funds*, Testimony Before the House Subcomm. on the Constitution, House Judiciary Comm., 107th Cong., 1st Sess. (June 7, 2001), *available at* <http://www. house.gov/judiciary/laycock>.

Douglas Laycock, *The Underlying Unity of Separation and Neutrality*, 46 Emory Law Journal 43 (1997).

Douglas Laycock, *Formal, Substantive, and Disaggregated Neutrality Toward Religion*, 39 DePaul Law Review 993 (1990).

Luis E. Lugo, *Equal Partners: The Welfare Responsibility of Governments and Churches* (1998).

Ira C. Lupu and Robert W. Tuttle, *Government Partnerships with Faith-Based Service Providers: The State of the Law* (Roundtable on Religion and Social Welfare Policy at the Rockefeller Institute of Government 2002), *available at* <www.religionandsocialpolicy. org/publications/ publication. cfm?id=22>.

Stephen V. Monsma, *When Sacred and Secular Mix: Religious Nonprofit Organizations and Public Money* (1996).

Stephen V. Monsma, *Putting Faith in Partnerships: Welfare-to-Work in Four Cities* (2004).

Office of Management and Budget, Executive Office of the President, *The President's Management Agenda* (fiscal year 2002) (Chapter 6 addresses OMB's efforts to advance the faith-based initiative).

Michael Stokes Paulsen, *A Funny Thing Happened on the Way to the Limited Public Forum: Unconstitutional Conditions on "Equal Access" for Religious Speakers and Groups*, 29 U. C. Davis Law Review 653 (1996).

Rebecca G. Rees, *"If We Recant, Would We Qualify?": Exclusion of Religious Providers from State Social Service Voucher Programs*, 56 Washington and Lee Law Review 1291 (1999).

Jeffrey Rosen, *Religious Rights: Why the Catholic Church Shouldn't Have to Hire Gays*, The New Republic, Feb. 26, 2001, at 16-17.

Amy L. Sherman, *The Charitable Choice Handbook for Ministry Leaders* (2001), *available at* <http://www.cpjustice.org/charitablechoice/publications>.

Amy L. Sherman, *Collaborations Catalogue: A Report on Charitable Choice Implementation in 15 States* (March 2002), *available at* <http://www.hudsonfaithincommunities.org>.

Ronald J. Sider, *Evaluating the Faith-Based Initiative: Is Charitable Choice Good Public Policy?* The Sorensen Lecture of Yale Divinity School (Oct. 15, 2002).

Ronald J. Sider, *The Case for "Discrimination,"* First Things, June-July, 2002, at 19-22.

Paul Taylor, *The Costs of Denying Religious Organizations the Right to Staff on a Religious Basis When They Join Federal Social Service Efforts*, 12 George Mason University Civil Rights Law Journal 159 (2002).

White House Office of Faith-Based and Community Initiatives, Executive Office of the President, *Protecting the Civil Rights and Religious Liberty of Faith-Based Organizations: Why Religious Hiring Rights Must Be Preserved* (June 23, 2003).

White House Office of Faith-Based and Community Initiatives, Executive Office of the President, *Guidance to Faith-Based and Community Organizations on Partnering with the Federal Government* (Dec. 12, 2002).

White House Office of Faith-Based and Community Initiatives, Executive Office of the President, *Unlevel Playing Field: Barriers to Participation by Faith-Based and Community Organizations in Federal Social Service Programs* (August 2001) (see especially pp. 15-17, numbering as barrier 5 the denial to faith-based organizations the ability to take religion into account in employment decisions).

Websites

The Center for Law and Religious Freedom of the Christian Legal Society <www.clsnet.org/clrfpages/>

The Center for Public Justice <www.cpjustice.org/charitablechoice>

The Faith in Communities Initiative of the Hudson Institute <www.hudsonfaithincommunities.org/fic/charitable.html>

The Faith and Service Technical Education Network (FASTEN) <www.fastennetwork.org>

The Roundtable on Religion and Social Welfare Policy <www.religionandsocialpolicy.org>

The White House Office of Faith-Based and Community Initiatives <www.whitehouse.gov/government/fbci/ >

Appendix 2.

Key Congressional and Executive Actions

Charitable Choice: Statutory and Regulatory Provisions

Charitable Choice Statutory Provisions for the Temporary Assistance for Needy Families (TANF) Program
Section 104 of The Personal Responsibility and Work Opportunity Reconciliation Act of 1996, Pub. L. No. 104-193, 110 Stat. 2105 (1996), (codified at 42 U.S.C. § 604a).

Charitable Choice Regulations for the TANF Program
Charitable Choice Provision Applicable to the Temporary Assistance for Needy Families Program, 68 Fed. Reg. 56449 (Sept. 30, 2003), (codified at 45 C.F.R. part 260).

Charitable Choice Statutory Provisions for the Community Services Block Grant (CSBG) Act.
Human Services Reauthorization Act of 1998, P. L. 105-285, Title II, Community Services Block Grant Program, §201 (Oct. 27, 1998), 112 Stat. 2749 (codified at 42 U.S.C. § 9920).

Charitable Choice Regulations for the CSBG Program
Charitable Choice Provisions Applicable to Programs Authorized Under the Community Services Block Grant Act, 68 Fed. Reg. 56466 (Sept. 30, 2003) (codified at 45 C.F.R. Part 1050).

Charitable Choice Statutory Provisions for Substance Abuse and Mental Health Services Administration (SAMHSA) Drug Treatment Programs
Charitable Choice for SAMHSA Drug Treatment Programs, from SAMHSA reauthorization through the Children's Health Act of 2000, P. L. 106-310, Title XXXIII, § 3305 (Oct. 17, 2000), 114 Stat. 1212 (codified at 42 U.S.C. § 300x-65).

Charitable Choice for SAMHSA Drug Treatment Programs (Dec. 2000), from Prevention and Treatment of Substance Abuse; Services Provided Through Religious Organizations, § 144 of H.R.

5662, Community Renewal Tax Relief Act of 2000, incorporated and enacted by reference in the Consolidated Appropriations Act, 2001, P. L. 106-554, §1 (Dec. 21, 2000), 114 Stat. 2783 (codified at 42 U.S.C. § 290kk).

Charitable Choice Regulations for SAMHSA Drug Treatment Programs
Charitable Choice Regulations applicable to States Receiving Substance Abuse Prevention and Treatment Block Grants, Projects for Assistance in Transition From Homelessness Formula Grants, and to Public and Private Providers Receiving Discretionary Grant Funding From SAMHSA for Provision of Substance Abuse Services Providing for Equal Treatment of SAMHSA Program Participants, 68 Fed. Reg. 56429 (Sept. 30, 2003) (codified at 42 C.F.R. Parts 54 and 54a).

Equal Treatment in Federally Funded Social-Service Programs Not Subject to Charitable Choice

Equal Protection Executive Order
Executive Order 13279, issued Dec. 12, 2003, *Equal Protection of the Laws for Faith-Based and Community Organizations and Permitting Religious Staffing by Faith-Based Federal Contractors*, 67 Fed. Reg. 77141 (Dec. 16, 2002).

US Agency for International Development Equal Treatment Regulations
Proposed Rule: Participation by Religious Organizations in USAID Programs, 69 Fed. Reg. 31773 (June 7, 2004) (to be codified at 21 C.F.R. Parts 201, 208, and 209).

Department of Agriculture Equal Treatment Regulations
Equal Opportunity for Religious Organizations, 69 Fed. Reg. 41375 (July 9, 2004) (codified at 7 C.F.R. Part 16).

Department of Education Equal Treatment Regulations
Participation in Education Department Programs by Religious Organizations; Providing for Equal Treatment of All Education

program Participants, 69 Fed. Reg. 31707 (June 4, 2004) (codified at 34 C.F.R. Parts 74, 75, 76, and 80).

Department of Health and Human Services Equal Treatment Regulations
Participation in Department of Health and Human Services Programs by Religious Organizations; Providing for Equal Treatment of All Department of Health and Human Services Program Participants, 69 Fed. Reg. 42586 (July 16, 2004) (codified at 45 C.F.R. Part 87).

Department of Housing and Urban Development Equal Treatment Regulations
Participation in HUD Programs by Faith-Based Organizations; Providing for Equal Treatment of all HUD Program Participants, 68 Fed. Reg. 56396 (Sept. 30, 2003) (codified at 24 C.F.R. Parts 92, 572, 574, 576, 582, 583, and 585).

Equal Participation of Faith-Based Organizations, 69 Fed. Reg. 41711 (July 9, 2004) (codified at 24 C.F.R. Part 5).

Proposed Rule: Participation in HUD's Native American Programs by Religious Organizations; Providing for Equal Treatment of All Program Participants, 69 Fed. Reg. 34543 (June 21, 2004) (to be codified at 24 C.F.R. Parts 954 and 1003).

Department of Justice Equal Treatment Regulations
Participation in Justice Department Programs by Religious Organizations; Providing for Equal Treatment of All Justice Department Program Participants, 69 Fed. Reg. 2832 (Jan. 21, 2004) (codified at 28 C.F.R. Part 38).

Department of Labor Equal Treatment Regulations
Limitation on Employment of Participants Under Title I of the Workforce Investment Act of 1998, 69 Fed. Reg. 41881 (July 12, 2004) (codified at 20 C.F.R. Part 667, and 29 C.F.R. Parts 2 and 37).

Office of Federal Contract Compliance Programs: Affirmative Action and Nondiscrimination Obligations of Government Contractors, Executive Order 11246, as amended; Exemption for Religious Entities, 68 Fed. Reg. 56392 (Sept. 30, 2003).

Department of Veterans Affairs Equal Treatment Regulations
VA Homeless Providers Grant and Per Diem Program; Religious Organizations, 69 Fed. Reg. 31883 (June 8, 2004) (codified at 38 C.F.R. Part 61).

Creating Federal Offices and Centers for Faith-Based and Community Initiatives

Executive Order 13198 (issued Jan. 29, 2001): Agency Responsibilities With Respect to Faith-Based and Community Initiatives, 66 Fed. Reg. 8497 (Jan. 31, 2001).

Executive Order 13199 (issued Jan. 29, 2001): Establishment of White House Office of Faith-Based and Community Initiatives, 66 Fed. Reg. 8499 (Jan. 31, 2001).

Executive Order 13280 (issued Dec. 12, 2002): Responsibilities of the Department of Agriculture and the Agency for International Development With Respect to Faith-Based and Community Initiatives, 67 Fed. Reg. 77145 (Dec. 16, 2002).

Executive Order 13342 (issued June 1, 2004): Responsibilities of the Departments of Commerce and Veterans Affairs and the Small Business Administration with Respect to Faith-Based and Community Initiatives, 69 Fed. Reg. 31509 (June 3, 2004).

Appendix 3.
Charitable Choice Provisions for the TANF Program

Sec. 604a: Services provided by charitable, religious, or private organizations

From Section 104 of the Personal Responsibility and Work Opportunity Reconciliation Act of 1996, Pub. L. No. 104-193, 110 Stat. 2105 (1996), (codified at 42 U.S.C. § 604a).

(a) IN GENERAL -

(1) STATE OPTIONS - A State may -

(A) administer and provide services under the programs described in subparagraphs (A) and (B)(i) of paragraph (2) through contracts with charitable, religious, or private organizations; and

(B) provide beneficiaries of assistance under the programs described in subparagraphs (A) and (B)(ii) of paragraph (2) with certificates, vouchers, or other forms of disbursement which are redeemable with such organizations.

(2) PROGRAMS DESCRIBED - The programs described in this paragraph are the following programs:

(A) A State program funded under this part (as amended by section 103(a) of this Act).

(B) Any other program established or modified under title I or II of this Act, that -

(i) permits contracts with organizations; or

(ii) permits certificates, vouchers, or other forms of disbursement to be provided to beneficiaries, as a means of providing assistance.

(b) RELIGIOUS ORGANIZATIONS - The purpose of this section is to allow States to contract with religious organizations, or to allow religious organizations to accept certificates, vouchers, or other forms of disbursement under any program described in subsection (a)(2) of this section, on the same basis as any other nongovernmental provider without impairing the religious character of such organizations, and without diminishing the religious freedom of beneficiaries of assistance funded under such program.

(c) NONDISCRIMINATION AGAINST RELIGIOUS ORGANIZATIONS - In the event a State exercises its authority under subsection (a) of this section, religious organizations are eligible, on the same basis as any other private organization, as contractors to provide assistance, or to accept certificates, vouchers, or other forms of disbursement, under any program described in subsection (a)(2) of this section so long as the programs are implemented consistent with the Establishment Clause of the United States Constitution. Except as provided in subsection (k) of this section, neither the Federal Government nor a State receiving funds under such programs shall discriminate against an organization which is or applies to be a contractor to provide assistance, or which accepts certificates, vouchers, or other forms of disbursement, on the basis that the organization has a religious character.

(d) RELIGIOUS CHARACTER AND FREEDOM -

(1) RELIGIOUS ORGANIZATIONS - A religious organization with a contract described in subsection (a)(1)(A) of this section, or which accepts certificates, vouchers, or other forms of disbursement under subsection (a)(1)(B) of this section, shall retain its independence from Federal, State, and local governments, including such organization's control over the definition, development, practice, and expression of its religious beliefs.

(2) ADDITIONAL SAFEGUARDS - Neither the Federal Government nor a State shall require a religious organization to

(A) alter its form of internal governance; or

(B) remove religious art, icons, scripture, or other symbols; in order to be eligible to contract to provide assistance, or to accept certificates, vouchers, or other forms of disbursement, funded under a program described in subsection (a)(2) of this section.

(e) RIGHTS OF BENEFICIARIES OF ASSISTANCE -

(1) IN GENERAL - If an individual described in paragraph (2) has an objection to the religious character of the organization or institution from which the individual receives, or would receive, assistance funded under any program described in subsection (a)(2) of this section, the State in which the individual resides shall provide such individual (if otherwise eligible for such assistance) within a reasonable period of time after the date of such objection with assistance from an alternative provider that is accessible to the individual and the value of which is not less than the value of the assistance which the individual would have received from such organization.

(2) INDIVIDUAL DESCRIBED - An individual described in this paragraph is an individual who receives, applies for, or requests to apply for, assistance under a program described in subsection (a)(2) of this section.

(f) EMPLOYMENT PRACTICES - A religious organization's exemption provided under section 2000e-1 of this title regarding employment practices shall not be affected by its participation in, or receipt of funds from, programs described in subsection (a)(2) of this section.

(g) NONDISCRIMINATION AGAINST BENEFICIARIES - Except as otherwise provided in law, a religious organization shall not discriminate against an individual in regard to rendering assistance funded under any program described in subsection (a)(2) of this section on the basis of religion, a religious belief, or refusal to actively participate in a religious practice.

(h) FISCAL ACCOUNTABILITY -

(1) IN GENERAL - Except as provided in paragraph (2), any religious organization contracting to provide assistance funded

under any program described in subsection (a)(2) of this section shall be subject to the same regulations as other contractors to account in accord with generally accepted auditing principles for the use of such funds provided under such programs.

(2) LIMITED AUDIT - If such organization segregates Federal funds provided under such programs into separate accounts, then only the financial assistance provided with such funds shall be subject to audit.

(i) COMPLIANCE - Any party which seeks to enforce its rights under this section may assert a civil action for injunctive relief exclusively in an appropriate State court against the entity or agency that allegedly commits such violation.

(j) LIMITATIONS ON USE OF FUNDS FOR CERTAIN PURPOSES - No funds provided directly to institutions or organizations to provide services and administer programs under subsection (a)(1)(A) of this section shall be expended for sectarian worship, instruction, or proselytization.

(k) PREEMPTION - Nothing in this section shall be construed to preempt any provision of a State constitution or State statute that prohibits or restricts the expenditure of State funds in or by religious organizations.

Appendix 4.
Charitable Choice Regulations for the TANF Program (Excerpts)

Charitable Choice Provisions Applicable to the Temporary Assistance for Needy Families Program, 68 Fed. Reg. 56449 (Sept. 30, 2003). Final Rule. Excerpts.

Department of Health and Human Services, Administration for Children and Families
Effective Date: October 30, 2003.

SUMMARY: This final rule implements the Charitable Choice statutory provisions in the Personal Responsibility and Work Opportunity Reconciliation Act of 1996 (PRWORA) as amended. The statutory and regulatory provisions apply to the Temporary Assistance for Needy Families (TANF) program administered by ACF. The statute and final rule establish requirements for State and local governments that administer or provide TANF services and benefits through contracts or through certificates, vouchers, or other forms of disbursement. The requirements and protections also apply to organizations, including faith-based organizations, that provide services and benefits with TANF funds and to the beneficiaries of those services.

The TANF Charitable Choice provisions of PRWORA were enacted to ensure that low-income families receive effective needed services, including services provided by faith-based organizations. In creating a Faith-Based and Community Initiative, President Bush has said: ". . . when we see social needs in America, my administration will look first to faith-based programs and community groups, which have proven their power to save and change lives. We will not fund the religious activities of any group. But when people of faith provide social services, we will not discriminate against them." To carry out that commitment and to implement the statute, the final rules clarify the protections for beneficiaries of services, the rights and obligations of religious organizations that provide TANF-funded services, and the requirements and limitations of State and local governments.

. . . .

[Response to Comments Received on the Proposed Rule]

I. CHARITABLE CHOICE STATUTORY FRAMEWORK

Title I of the Personal Responsibility and Work Opportunity Reconciliation Act of 1996 (PRWORA) (Pub. L. 104-193) sets forth certain "Charitable Choice" provisions in section 104, entitled "Services Provided By Charitable, Religious, or Private Organizations." This section clarifies State authority to administer and provide TANF services through contracts with charitable, religious, or private organizations and to provide beneficiaries with certificates, vouchers, or other forms of disbursement, which are redeemable with such organizations. The provisions of section 104 are hereinafter referred to as "TANF Charitable Choice provisions." In addition to giving States the ability to contract with a range of service providers and use optimal funding mechanisms, and giving families a greater choice of TANF-funded providers, section 104 sets forth certain requirements to ensure that religious organizations are able to compete on an equal footing for funds under the TANF program, without impairing the religious character of such organizations or diminishing the religious freedom of TANF beneficiaries.

President Bush has made it one of his Administration's top priorities to ensure that Federal programs are fully open to faith-based and community groups in a manner that is consistent with the Constitution. It is the Administration's view that faith-based organizations are an indispensable part of the social services network of the United States. Faith-based organizations, including places of worship, non-profit organizations, and neighborhood groups, offer a myriad of social services to those in need. The TANF Charitable Choice provisions are consistent with the Administration's belief that there should be an equal opportunity for all organizations—both faith-based and non-religious—to participate as partners in Federal programs to serve Americans in need.

This final rule implements the TANF Charitable Choice provisions applicable to State and local governments and to religious organizations in their use of Federal TANF and State maintenance-of-effort (MOE) funds. The objective of this rule is to ensure that the TANF program is open to all eligible organizations, regardless of their religious affiliation or character, and to establish clearly the proper uses to which funds may be put and the conditions for receipt of funding.

This final rule adds Sec. 260.34, "When do the Charitable Choice provisions of TANF apply?" to 45 CFR Part 260, "General Temporary Assistance For Needy Families Provisions." The introductory language addresses the applicability of the Charitable Choice provisions to the TANF program . . . .

Specifically, the rules provide that Charitable Choice applies whenever a State or local government:

- Uses Federal TANF funds or expends State or local funds claimed to meet the State's MOE requirement to procure services and benefits from non-governmental organizations; or,

- Provides clients with certificates, vouchers, or other forms of disbursement that can be redeemed for services in connection with the TANF program.

When State or local funds are used to meet the TANF MOE requirements, the provisions apply irrespective of whether the State or local funds are commingled with Federal funds, segregated, or expended in separate State programs. However, pursuant to section 104(k) of PRWORA as amended (42 U.S.C. 604a(k)), nothing in the Charitable Choice requirements shall be construed to preempt any provision of a State constitution or State statute that prohibits or restricts the expenditure of State funds in or by religious organizations. Accordingly, States that are subject to such restrictions should segregate their Federal funds from the funds which are subject to the provisions of the statute.

The word "assistance" is used throughout the Charitable Choice provisions in section 104 of PRWORA as amended (42 U.S.C. 604a). When "assistance" is used in the Charitable Choice statutory provisions, it broadly refers to all kinds of help, services, and benefits. In other words, it is broader than the definition of "assistance" under 45 CFR 260.31(a) of this part. The Charitable Choice provisions apply to any and all of the services and benefits available to clients, through contracts, certificates, vouchers, or other forms of disbursement of TANF funds. Thus, we have used the term "benefits" and "services" in the final regulation to refer to the broad range of activities or help available to clients. We also want to avoid any misunderstanding that Charitable Choice is solely limited to the provision of the types of services that constitute "assistance" as defined in 45 CFR 260.31(a).

However, because the Charitable Choice provisions refer only to State and local governments, Sec. 260.34 does not apply to Tribal governments operating TANF programs under section 412 of the Social Security Act.

. . . .

IV. EQUAL TREATMENT FOR RELIGIOUS ORGANIZATIONS

Background: Under Sec. 260.34(a)(2) of the proposed rule (Sec. 260.34(b)(2)), we clarified that organizations are eligible to participate in the TANF program without regard to their religious character or affiliation, and may not be excluded because they are religious. Federal, State and local governments administering TANF funds are prohibited from discriminating against organizations on the basis of religion or their religious character.

. . . .

VI. RELIGIOUS CHARACTER AND INDEPENDENCE OF RELIGIOUS ORGANIZATIONS

Background: Section 260.34(d) of the final rule clarifies that a religious organization that participates in the TANF program retains its independence from Federal, State, and local governments, provided that it does not use direct Federal TANF or MOE funds to support inherently religious activities. It may continue to carry out its mission, including the definition, practice and expression of its religious beliefs. Among other things, religious organizations may use their facilities to provide TANF-funded services, without removing religious art, icons, scriptures, or other symbols. In addition, a religious organization that receives Federal TANF or State MOE funds may retain religious terms in its organization's name, select its board members on a religious basis, and include religious references in its organization's mission statements and other governing documents.

Comment: A number of commenters expressed concern that a religious organization in receipt of Federal TANF or State MOE funds does not have to remove the religious art, icons, scriptures, or other symbols. The commenters think that this provision is too broad. It could result in the organization providing services in a setting that may well constitute a "pervasively sectarian" atmosphere in which members of a different religion may not feel comfortable or welcome to receive their TANF-funded benefits. For example, the organization could conduct the government-funded program in a chapel, leading to a reasonable misperception of government endorsement of or support for religion.

Response: Section 104(d) of PRWORA as amended (42 U.S.C. 604a(d)) imposes on the government a duty not to intrude into the institutional autonomy of religious organizations. Each participating faith-based organization in receipt of Federal TANF or State MOE funds, whether directly or indirectly, shall retain its independence from Federal, State and local governments. This independence includes their control over the definition, development, practice, and expression of its religious beliefs. In addition, the statute expressly prohibits State, Federal, and local governments from requiring a religious organization to alter its form of internal governance or to remove religious art, icons, scripture, or other symbols in order to be eligible to receive directly or indirectly funded Federal TANF or State MOE funds to provide help to beneficiaries. If the beneficiary objects to the religious character, then he or she is entitled to receive the social service benefit at an alternate provider to which the beneficiary has no religious objection. In addition, as noted above, the Supreme Court's "pervasively sectarian" doctrine no longer enjoys the support of a majority of the Court. See *Mitchell v. Helms*, 530 U.S. 793, 825-829 (2000) (plurality opinion), *id.* At 857.858 (O'Connor, J.) (requiring proof of "actual diversion of public support to religious uses").

Comment: Several commenters noted that the protections afforded in this subsection are consistent with the statute and should be maintained. One of the commenters requested that we add a statement essentially stating that "contrary State and local procurement laws that would otherwise prohibit faith-based organizations (FBOs) from continuing to staff on a religious basis" are preempted. Another commenter asked that we add language essentially stating that nothing in this section shall be construed to affect any State or local law or regulation that relates to discrimination in employment, including the provision of employee benefits.

Response: The protections in Sec. 260.34(d) have been retained. We believe that the content of this subsection suffices as written.

As discussed under "Employment Practices," the FBOs enjoy an exemption "with respect to the employment of individuals of a particular religion," under Title VII of the Federal Civil Rights Act of 1964. Therefore, in keeping with the guarantees of institutional autonomy, a religious organization may continue to select its own staff in a manner that takes into account its faith, without violating Title VII.

The Charitable Choice provision at section 104(f) of PRWORA as amended (42 U.S.C. 604a(f)) expressly guarantees that a religious organization's Title VII exemption shall not be affected by its participation in or receipt of TANF funds, whether the State or local government directly or indirectly uses Federal TANF funds or expends State or local funds claimed to meet the State's MOE requirement to pay for the services.

. . . .

VII. EMPLOYMENT PRACTICES

Background: In language similar to that in the statute, the proposed rule at Sec. 260.34(d) (now Sec. 260.34(e)) specified that the receipt of TANF or MOE funds does not affect a participating religious organization's exemption provided under 42 U.S.C. 2000-e regarding employment practices. Title VII of the Federal Civil Rights Act of 1964 permits a religious organization to hire employees who share its religious beliefs. This helps enable faith-based groups to promote common values, a unity of purpose, and shared service—thus protecting the religious liberty of communities of faith.

Comment: Several commenters agreed that the proposed rule reflects a proper understanding of civil rights law. When a faith-based organization receives government funding and hires staff on a religious basis, the law is not violated.

Response: We agree with these commenters and have retained the identical language in the final rule. This statutory and regulatory provision of

Charitable Choice does not change the status quo; it simply clarifies the applicability of the exemption to the TANF program.

Comment: Several commenters believed that the proposed rule allows employment discrimination in violation of constitutional prohibitions and court decisions that have struck down government-funded discrimination. One commenter explicitly stated that this provision runs afoul of the "no-religious-tests clause" of the Constitution under which "no religious test shall ever be required as a qualification to any office or public trust under the United States."

Response: We do not agree with these commenters. The Equal Employment Opportunity Act of 1972 broadened Title VII of the Civil Rights Act of 1964 to free religious organizations from charges of religious discrimination, regardless of the nature of the job. In 1987 the Supreme Court addressed and unanimously upheld the constitutionality of the 1972 amendment or exemption for religious organizations. In addition, it is well settled that the receipt of government funds does not convert the employment decisions of private institutions into "state action" that is subject to constitutional restrictions such as the "no religious test" clause of the Constitution.

Comment: A number of commenters stated that the exemption from Title VII of the Civil Rights Act was never intended to permit a religious organization to favor co-religionists in hiring when using Federal funds to pay the salaries and wages of employees who are carrying out governmentally-funded social service programs.

Response: We do not agree that these comments accurately portray the law. Title VII of the Civil Rights Act, which applies to organizations regardless of whether they receive Federal funds, contains an explicit exemption for religious organizations, which allows them to hire, promote, and fire staff on a basis that takes into consideration the organization's religious beliefs and practices without violating Title VII. That exemption is not lost when a faith-based organization receives Federal TANF funds or State MOE funds to provide a secular service. Also, we would note that section 702(a) of the Civil Rights Act of 1964 is permissive. It allows religious staffing, but does not require it. And, religious organizations are subject to Federal civil rights laws that prohibit employment discrimination on the basis of race, color, national origin, sex, age, and disability.

Comment: Several commenters noted that State and local governments have contracting laws that prohibit employment discrimination, beyond the Civil Rights Act of 1964. These commenters asked that the final rule clarify that nothing in the rule is intended to modify or affect any State law or regulation that relates to discrimination in employment.

Response: The Charitable Choice provision at section 104(f) of PRWORA as amended (42 U.S.C. 604a(f)) expressly guarantees that a religious organization's Title VII exemption shall not be affected by its participation in or receipt of TANF funds. Hence, Charitable Choice applies whenever a State or local government uses Federal TANF funds or expends State or local funds claimed to meet the State's MOE requirement to procure services and benefits from non-governmental organizations, or provides clients with certificates, vouchers, or other forms of disbursement that can be redeemed for services in connection with the TANF program. When State or local funds are used to meet the State's MOE requirement, the provisions apply irrespective of whether the State or local funds are commingled with Federal funds, segregated, or expended in separate State programs.

The only exception is found in section 104(k) of PRWORA as amended (42 U.S.C.604a(k)), which clarifies that the Charitable Choice requirements do not preempt any provision of a State constitution or State statute that prohibits or restricts the expenditure of State funds in or by religious organizations. We do not believe that this "preemption" provision can be interpreted to cover State or local employment discrimination laws. (For a more detailed analysis of the implications of Charitable Choice on State and local laws, see the analysis provided under the heading "Effect on State and Local Funds".)

. . . .

XI. EFFECT ON STATE AND LOCAL FUNDS

Background: Section 104(a) of PRWORA as amended (42 U.S.C. 604a(a)) applies to "a State program funded under part A of title IV of the Social Security Act" (TANF) and also to "any other program established or modified under title I or title II of this Act that permits contracts with organizations; or permits certificates, vouchers, or other forms of disbursement to be provided to beneficiaries as a means of providing assistance." Title I includes all TANF provisions, including the maintenance-of-effort (MOE) requirement that States continue to expend a specified level of State or local funds. Claimed expenditures must be spent on eligible families for activities that achieve a TANF purpose. (Title II is the Supplemental Security Income program.)

The proposed rule followed the statute in specifying that the Charitable Choice requirements apply both when a State or local government uses Federal TANF funds to procure services and benefits from non-governmental organizations, or to redeem certificates, vouchers, or other forms of disbursement or when the State claims those expenditures to meet the MOE requirement. We said that the Charitable Choice provisions apply whether the State or local funds are commingled with Federal funds, segregated, or expended in separate State programs.

The proposed rule also clarified that, pursuant to section 104(k) of PRWORA as amended (42 U.S.C. 604a(k)), nothing in the Charitable Choice requirements shall be construed to preempt any provision of a State constitution or State statute that prohibits or restricts the expenditure of State funds in or by religious organizations.

Comment: A number of commenters opposed the application of Charitable Choice to the State and local funds claimed to meet the MOE requirement. Some believed that Charitable Choice should only apply to the use of Federal TANF dollars. Others believed that the rule covers commingled funds, but asked that we modify the rule with respect to both segregated funds and funds expended in separate State programs. Still others believed the rule should apply to funds expended in the TANF program (Federal funds, commingled and segregated MOE expenditures) but that it ought not apply to expenditures in separate State programs, like other TANF rules.

Response: Because ACF did not regulate on Charitable Choice or provide guidance earlier, we recognize that many may not have understood that the statutory provision applies to State and local funds claimed to meet the State's MOE requirement, just as it applies to Federal TANF funds. Given the nearly total flexibility provided to States with respect to separate State programs, we also acknowledge that the application of the Charitable Choice requirements to these funds is unusual, because only a few of the TANF rules apply to the expenditure of State funds in separate State programs.

But, while we recognize the frustration of some of the commenters with the interpretation in the NPRM and the preference of others to modify the rule, for the reasons explained in the "Background" above, we believe the better reading of the statute is that Charitable Choice applies to all State funds claimed to meet the maintenance-of-effort requirements.

Comment: Several commenters noted that the preemption clause did not address local laws and asked us to clarify in the final rule that the Charitable Choice provisions do not preempt any provision of a State constitution, State statute or local ordinances that prohibits or restricts the expenditure of State funds in or by religious organizations.

Response: Section 104(k) (42 U.S.C. 604a(k)) preserves "a State constitution or State statute that prohibits or restricts the expenditure of State funds in or by religious organizations"; it contains no reference to "local laws" or "ordinances." In addition, the TANF Charitable Choice statute, read as a whole, demonstrates that Congress was cognizant of the distinction between State and local law. For example, section 104(d)(1) (42 U.S.C. 604a(d)(1)) provides that a religious organization participating in a TANF program "shall retain its independence from Federal, State, and local governments . . . ." We therefore believe that the existing language faithfully implements the statute.

Comment: Several commenters noted that the proposed rule was confusing. If Charitable Choice applies to the use of Federal funds and all State and local expenditures claimed to meet MOE, what does the preemption provision mean?

Response: We understand the confusion. But, Congress recognized that some States have enacted laws to ensure a more rigorous "separation of church and state." These States either prohibit or restrict contracts with religious organizations or more broadly proscribe providing any State funding to them. In enacting Charitable Choice, Congress explicitly allowed these State prohibitions or restrictions, as they apply to State funds only, to take precedence over this Federal provision.

The provision at section 104(k) of PRWORA as amended (42 U.S.C. 604a(k)) which preserves "a State constitution or State statute that prohibits or restricts the expenditure of State funds in or by religious organizations," only applies to the State's own funds, but not to Federal TANF funds. The "preemption" provision also does not apply to State funds that have been commingled with Federal TANF funds. (Federal requirements only affect the use of Federal TANF funds, unless the State commingles its money with

Federal TANF funds. If a State commingles its funds, the Federal and State funds become subject to the same rules.) A number of States may have general or specific provisions that prohibit or restrict providing direct or indirect State funds to religious organizations. Such States should use segregated Federal TANF funds to pay for any benefits and services provided by religious organizations, to avoid the risk of running afoul of a provision in their laws that prohibits or restricts the expenditure of State funds in or by religious organizations.

So, another way of expressing the requirements is that if a State's constitution or law prohibits or restricts State funds from going to religious organizations, or proscribes contracts with religious organizations, the Charitable Choice requirements do not apply to those State funds. We defer to the State to interpret the scope of its constitution or law. But, if a State does not have such prohibitions or restrictions, then Charitable Choice applies to both Federal TANF funds and State and local expenditures claimed for MOE purposes. This is faithful to Congress' expressed intention to preserve State constitutional or statutory restrictions on State funds, while ensuring that Federal rules apply to both Federal and State MOE funds in the absence of such State law provisions.

Comment: Several commenters asked that the final rule clarify that the provision at section 104(k) of PRWORA as amended (42 U.S.C. 604a(k)) which preserves "a State constitution or State statute that prohibits or restricts the expenditure of State funds in or by religious organizations," also includes State and local nondiscrimination hiring provisions.

Response: We do not agree that the provision at section 104(k) of PRWORA as amended (42 U.S.C. 604a(k)) addresses employment nondiscrimination provisions. Rather, this provision explicitly covers provisions of a State constitution or State statute that prohibits or restricts the expenditure of State funds "in or by religious organizations." Employment nondiscrimination provisions do not fall within this category.

. . . .

XIII. Regulatory Analysis

. . . .

Regulatory Flexibility Analysis

. . . .

Comment: One commenter stated that the rule should be considered "major" because it will have a significantly adverse impact on employment by allowing for discrimination based on religion.

Response: We disagree. For years, section 702(a) of the Civil Rights Act of 1964 as amended has relieved religious organization from compliance with Title VII employment nondiscrimination requirements. Therefore, we believe that there will not be any significant adverse impact on employment.

. . . .

SEC. 260.34. WHEN DO THE CHARITABLE CHOICE PROVISIONS OF TANF APPLY?

(a) These Charitable Choice provisions apply whenever a State or local government uses Federal TANF funds or expends State and local funds used to meet maintenance-of-effort (MOE) requirements of the TANF program to directly procure services and benefits from non-governmental organizations, or provides TANF beneficiaries with certificates, vouchers, or other forms of indirect disbursement redeemable from such organizations . . . .

(b) (1) Religious organizations are eligible, on the same basis as any other organization, to participate in TANF as long as their Federal TANF or State MOE funded services are provided consistent with the Establishment Clause and the Free Exercise Clause of the First Amendment to the United States Constitution.

(2) Neither the Federal government nor a State or local government in its use of Federal TANF or State MOE funds shall, in the selection of service providers, discriminate for or against an organization that applies to provide, or provides TANF services or benefits on the basis of the organization's religious character or affiliation.

. . . .

(d) A religious organization that participates in the TANF program will retain its independence from Federal, State, and local governments and may continue to carry out its mission, including the definition, practice and expression of its religious beliefs, provided that it does not expend Federal TANF or State MOE funds that it receives directly to support any inherently religious activities, such as worship, religious instruction, or proselytization. Among other things, faith-based organizations may use space in their facilities to provide TANF-funded services without removing religious art, icons, scriptures, or other symbols. In addition, a Federal TANF or State MOE funded religious organization retains the authority over its internal governance, and it may retain religious terms in its organization's name, select its board members on a religious basis, and include religious references in its organization's mission statements and other governing documents.

(e) The participation of a religious organization in, or its receipt of funds from, a TANF program does not affect that organization's exemption provided under 42 U.S.C. 2000e-1 regarding employment practices.

. . . .

(i) This section applies whenever a State or local organization uses Federal TANF or State MOE funds to procure services and benefits from non-governmental organizations, or redeems certificates, vouchers, or other forms of disbursement from them whether with Federal funds, or State and local funds claimed to meet the MOE requirements of section 409(a)(7) of the Social Security Act. Subject to the requirements of paragraph (j), when State or local funds are used to meet the TANF MOE requirements, the provisions apply irrespective of whether the State or local funds are commingled with Federal funds, segregated, or expended in separate State programs.

(j) Preemption. Nothing in this section shall be construed to preempt any provision of a State constitution, or State statute that prohibits or restricts the expenditure of segregated or separate State funds in or by religious organizations.

. . . .

(l) Any party which seeks to enforce its right under this section may assert a civil action for injunctive relief exclusively in an appropriate State court against the entity or agency that allegedly commits such violation.

Appendix 5.
Charitable Choice Regulations for SAMHSA Programs (Excerpts)

Charitable Choice Regulations Applicable to States Receiving Substance Abuse Prevention and Treatment Block Grants, Projects for Assistance in Transition From Homelessness Formula Grants, and to Public and Private Providers Receiving Discretionary Grant Funding From SAMHSA for the Provision of Substance Abuse Services Providing for Equal Treatment of SAMHSA Program Participants, 68 Fed. Reg. 56429 (Sept. 30, 2003). Final Rule. Excerpts.

Department of Health and Human Services, Substance Abuse and Mental Health Services Administration
Effective Date: October 30, 2003.

SUMMARY: On December 17, 2002, the Department of Health and Human Services (HHS) published a Notice of Proposed Rulemaking (NPRM) to implement the Charitable Choice statutory provisions of the Public Health Service Act, applicable to the Substance Abuse Prevention and Treatment (SAPT) Block Grant program, the Projects for Assistance in Transition from Homelessness (PATH) formula grant program, insofar as recipients provide substance abuse services, and to SAMHSA discretionary grants for substance abuse treatment or prevention services, which are all administered by the Substance Abuse and Mental Health Services Administration (SAMHSA) of the U.S. Department of Health and Human Services . . . .

. . . .

RESPONSE TO COMMENTS RECEIVED ON THE PROPOSED RULE

. . . .

EMPLOYMENT PRACTICES (Sec. 54.6 and 54a.6)

The NPRM restated the SAMHSA's Charitable Choice provisions, which provide that a religious organization's exemption provided under section 702 of the Civil Rights Act of 1964 regarding employment practices shall not be affected by its participation in, or receipt of funds from, a designated program. To the extent that 42 U.S.C. 300x-57(a)(2) or 42 U.S.C. 290cc-33(a)(2) imposes religious nondiscrimination requirements on the employment practices of program participants, the NPRM clarifies that such requirements do not apply to program participants that demonstrate that these requirements would substantially burden their exercise of religion.

Comments: Numerous comments were received dealing with the employment practices provisions in the proposed rule. Nineteen out of 23 comments made about this provision supported the removal of the provision from the final rule. Many commenters felt that the Religious Freedom Restoration Act (RFRA) was an inappropriate basis for the regulation and did not provide the statutory authority to overrule the broad anti-discrimination provision in SAMHSA's authorizing legislation for the Substance Abuse Prevention and Treatment (SAPT) block grant in the Public Health Service Act. They argued that religious groups would not be substantially burdened by having to comply with these requirements, and that, in any event, the government had a compelling interest in imposing the requirements.

Response: The Department does not agree with the comments. We believe that, in addition to being a reasonable construction of the SAMHSA Charitable Choice provision, the inapplicability of the discrimination provisions of the SAPT block grant program and the PATH program, 42 U.S.C. 300x-57(a)(2) and 42 U.S.C. 290cc-33(a)(2), to religious organizations that demonstrate a substantial burden on their exercise of religion follows from RFRA. Under RFRA, the government may not impose legal requirements that substantially burden a grantee's exercise of religion unless doing so is the least restrictive means of furthering a compelling government interest. 42 U.S.C. 2000bb-1(b). Accordingly, where a religious entity establishes that its exercise of religion would be substantially burdened by the religious nondiscrimination provisions cited above, RFRA supercedes those statutory requirements, thus exempting the religious entity there from, unless the Department has a compelling interest in enforcing them.

The Department's rationale in this regard is set out in the NPRM. See 67 FR 77350, 77351-77352 (Dec. 17, 2002). Several points, however, merit elaboration. First, the Department recognizes that not all religious organizations that might receive funding under the SAPT block grant and PATH programs would be substantially burdened by the application of the religious nondiscrimination requirements of 42 U.S.C. 300x-57(a)(2) and 42 U.S.C. 290cc-33(a)(2). For example, some religious organizations are concerned only with their employees' commitment to providing social services, not with any profession of faith, and thus do not consider religion in hiring people to perform such services. Such groups would not likely be burdened by having to comply with a religious nondiscrimination requirement. Many other religious organizations, however, consider religious faith critical to all of their employees' activities, including those that involve providing government-funded social services to the public. For these groups, imposition of a religious nondiscrimination requirement can impose a particularly harsh burden. As Justice Brennan explained: "Determining that certain activities are in furtherance of an organization's religious mission, and that only those committed to that mission should conduct them, is . . . a means by which a religious community defines itself." *Corporation of Presiding Bishop v. Amos*, 483 U.S. 327, 342 (1987) (Brennan, J., concurring). For groups that deem religious faith an important part of their self-definition, having to make employment decisions without regard to their faith would substantially alter the charter of their organization.

In recognition that the religious nondiscrimination requirements of 42 U.S.C. 300x-57(a)(2) and 42 U.S.C. 290cc-33(a)(2) would substantially burden some but not other grantees, the RFRA exemption is limited to those organizations that are able to certify that: (1) They sincerely believe that employing individuals of a particular religion is important to the definition and maintenance of their religious identity, autonomy, and/or communal religious exercise; (2) they make employment decisions on a religious basis in analogous programs; (3) the grant in question would materially affect their ability to provide the type of services in question; and (4) providing the services in question is expressive of their values or mission. We disagree, however, with some commenters' assertion that no religious organization would be substantially burdened by having to make hiring decisions without regard to their faith while participating in the SAMHSA program.

Second, the fact that SAMHSA is a funding program does not mean that the Federal government necessarily possesses a "compelling interest" in imposing religious nondiscrimination provisions upon the employment practices of participating religious organizations. To begin with, religious organizations' exemption from the religious nondiscrimination requirements of Title VII (the availability of that exemption is expressly clarified by the SAMHSA Charitable Choice law, 42 U.S.C. 290kk-1(e), 300x-65(d)(2)) reflects Congress's judgment that employment decisions are an important component of religious organizations' autonomy, and that the government has a much stronger interest in applying a religious nondiscrimination requirement to secular organizations than to religious organizations[,] many of whose existence depends upon their ability to define themselves on a religious basis. Moreover, many federal funding programs—including the discretionary grant programs administered by the Secretary under Title V of the Public Health Service Act—do not impose a religious nondiscrimination requirement upon the employment practices of grantees. Rather, Congress's application of religious nondiscrimination requirements in the employment context is quite selective, which makes it difficult to regard the government as having a compelling interest in imposing such a requirement in this particular context. Finally, secular entities that administer federally funded social programs generally are not barred from considering their ideologies in making employment decisions. In this respect, allowing faith-based grantees to consider religious motivation in hiring simply levels the playing field, allowing them to consider ideology on the same basis as other organizations.

. . . .

PART 54—CHARITABLE CHOICE REGULATIONS APPLICABLE TO STATES RECEIVING SUBSTANCE ABUSE PREVENTION AND TREATMENT BLOCK GRANTS AND/OR PROJECTS FOR ASSISTANCE IN TRANSITION FROM HOMELESSNESS GRANTS

. . . .

SEC. 54.6 EMPLOYMENT PRACTICES

(a) The participation of a religious organization in, or its receipt of funds from, an applicable program does not affect that organization's exemption provided under 42 U.S.C. 2000e-1 regarding employment practices.

(b) To the extent that 42 U.S.C. 300x-57(a)(2) or 42 U.S.C. 290cc-33(a)(2) precludes a program participant from employing individuals of a particular religion to perform work connected with the carrying on of its activities, those provisions do not apply if such program participant is a religious corporation, association, educational institution, or society and can demonstrate that its religious exercise would be substantially burdened by application of these religious nondiscrimination requirements to its employment practices in the program or activity at issue. In order to make this demonstration, the program participant must certify: that it sincerely believes that employing individuals of a particular religion is important to the definition and maintenance of its religious identity, autonomy, and/or communal religious exercise; that it makes employment decisions on a religious basis in analogous programs; that the grant would materially affect its ability to provide the type of services in question; and that providing the services in question is expressive of its values or mission. The organization must maintain documentation to support these determinations and must make such documentation available to SAMHSA upon request.

(c) Nothing in this section shall be construed to modify or affect any State law or regulation that relates to discrimination in employment.

(d) The phrases "with respect to the employment," "individuals of a particular religion," and "religious corporation, association, educational institution, or society" shall have the same meaning as those terms have under section 702 of the Civil Rights Act of 1964, 42 U.S.C. 2000e-1(a).

. . . .

Appendix 6.
Executive Order 13279,
Equal Protection of the Laws

Executive Order 13279 of December 12, 2002, *Equal Protection of the Laws for Faith-Based and Community Organizations*, 67 Fed. Reg. 77141 (Dec. 16, 2002).

By the authority vested in me as President by the Constitution and the laws of the United States of America, including section 121(a) of title 40, United States Code, and section 301 of title 3, United States Code, and in order to guide Federal agencies in formulating and developing policies with implications for faith-based organizations and other community organizations, to ensure equal protection of the laws for faith-based and community organizations, to further the national effort to expand opportunities for, and strengthen the capacity of, faith-based and other community organizations so that they may better meet social needs in America's communities, and to ensure the economical and efficient administration and completion of Government contracts, it is hereby ordered as follows:

SEC. 1. DEFINITIONS - For purposes of this order:

(a) "Federal financial assistance" means assistance that non-Federal entities receive or administer in the form of grants, contracts, loans, loan guarantees, property, cooperative agreements, food commodities, direct appropriations, or other assistance, but does not include a tax credit, deduction, or exemption.

(b) "Social service program" means a program that is administered by the Federal Government, or by a State or local government using Federal financial assistance, and that provides services directed at reducing poverty, improving opportunities for low-income children, revitalizing low-income communities, empowering low-income families and low-income individuals to become self-sufficient, or otherwise helping people in need. Such programs include, but are not limited to, the following:

(i) child care services, protective services for children and adults, services for children and adults in foster care, adoption services, services related to the management and maintenance of the home, day care services for adults, and services to meet the special needs of children, older individuals, and individuals with disabilities (including physical, mental, or emotional disabilities);

(ii) transportation services;

(iii) job training and related services, and employment services;

(iv) information, referral, and counseling services;

(v) the preparation and delivery of meals and services related to soup kitchens or food banks;

(vi) health support services;

(vii) literacy and mentoring programs;

(viii)services for the prevention and treatment of juvenile delinquency and substance abuse, services for the prevention of crime and the provision of assistance to the victims and the families of criminal offenders, and services related to intervention in, and prevention of, domestic violence; and

(ix) services related to the provision of assistance for housing under Federal law.

(c) "Policies that have implications for faith-based and community organizations" refers to all policies, programs, and regulations, including official guidance and internal agency procedures, that have significant effects on faith-based organizations participating in or seeking to participate in social service programs supported with Federal financial assistance.

(d) "Agency" means a department or agency in the executive branch.

(e) "Specified agency heads" mean the Attorney General, the Secretaries of Agriculture, Education, Health and Human Services, Housing and Urban Development, and Labor, and the Administrator of the Agency for International Development.

SEC. 2. FUNDAMENTAL PRINCIPLES AND POLICYMAKING CRITERIA -

In formulating and implementing policies that have implications for faith-based and community organizations, agencies that administer social service programs supported with Federal financial assistance shall, to the extent permitted by law, be guided by the following fundamental principles:

(a) Federal financial assistance for social service programs should be distributed in the most effective and efficient manner possible;

(b) The Nation's social service capacity will benefit if all eligible organizations, including faith-based and other community organizations, are able to compete on an equal footing for Federal financial assistance used to support social service programs;

(c) No organization should be discriminated against on the basis of religion or religious belief in the administration or distribution of Federal financial assistance under social service programs;

(d) All organizations that receive Federal financial assistance under social services programs should be prohibited from discriminating against beneficiaries or potential beneficiaries of the social services programs on the basis of religion or religious belief. Accordingly, organizations, in providing services supported in whole or in part with Federal financial assistance, and in their outreach activities related to such services, should not be allowed to discriminate against current or prospective program beneficiaries on the basis of religion, a religious belief, a refusal to hold a religious belief, or a refusal to actively participate in a religious practice;

(e) The Federal Government must implement Federal programs in accordance with the Establishment Clause and the Free Exercise Clause of the First Amendment to the Constitution. Therefore, organizations that engage in inherently religious activities, such as worship, religious instruction, and proselytization, must offer those services separately in time or location from any programs or services supported with direct Federal financial assistance, and participation in any such inherently religious activities must be voluntary for the beneficiaries of the social service program supported with such Federal financial assistance; and

(f) Consistent with the Free Exercise Clause and the Free Speech Clause of the Constitution, faith-based organizations should be eligible to compete for Federal financial assistance used to support social service programs and to participate fully in the social service programs supported with Federal financial assistance without impairing their independence, autonomy, expression, or religious character. Accordingly, a faith-based organization that applies for or participates in a social service program supported with Federal financial assistance may retain its independence and may continue to carry out its mission, including the definition, development, practice, and expression of its religious beliefs, provided that it does not use direct Federal financial assistance to support any inherently religious activities, such as worship, religious instruction, or proselytization. Among other things, faith-based organizations that receive Federal financial assistance may use their facilities to provide social services supported with Federal financial assistance, without removing or altering religious art, icons, scriptures, or other symbols from these facilities. In addition, a faith-based organization that applies for or participates in a social service program supported with Federal financial assistance may retain religious terms in its organization's name, select its board members on a religious basis, and include religious references in its organization's mission statements and other chartering or governing documents.

SEC. 3. AGENCY IMPLEMENTATION -

(a) Specified agency heads shall, in coordination with the White House Office of Faith-Based and Community Initiatives (White House OFBCI), review and evaluate existing policies that have implications for faith-based and community organizations in order to assess the consistency of such policies with the fundamental principles and policymaking criteria articulated in section 2 of this order.

(b) Specified agency heads shall ensure that all policies that have implications for faith-based and community organizations are consistent with the fundamental principles and policymaking criteria articulated in section 2 of this order. Therefore, specified agency heads shall, to the extent permitted by law:

(i) amend all such existing policies of their respective agencies to ensure that they are consistent with the fundamental principles and policymaking criteria articulated in section 2 of this order;

(ii) where appropriate, implement new policies for their respective agencies that are consistent with and necessary to further the fundamental principles and policymaking criteria set forth in section 2 of this order; and

(iii) implement new policies that are necessary to ensure that their respective agencies collect data regarding the participation of faith-based and community organizations in social service programs that receive Federal financial assistance.

(c) Within 90 days after the date of this order, each specified agency head shall report to the President, through the Director of the White House OFBCI, the actions it proposes to undertake to accomplish the activities set forth in sections 3(a) and (b) of this order.

SEC. 4. AMENDMENT OF EXECUTIVE ORDER 11246 -

Pursuant to section 121(a) of title 40, United States Code, and section 301 of title 3, United States Code, and in order to further the strong Federal interest in ensuring that the cost and progress of Federal procurement contracts are not adversely affected by an artificial restriction of the labor pool caused by the unwarranted exclusion of faith-based organizations from such contracts, section 204 of Executive Order 11246 of September 24, 1965, as amended, is hereby further amended to read as follows:

"SEC. 204 (a) The Secretary of Labor may, when the Secretary deems that special circumstances in the national interest so require, exempt a contracting agency from the requirement of including any or all of the provisions of Section 202 of this Order in any specific contract, subcontract, or purchase order.

(b) The Secretary of Labor may, by rule or regulation, exempt certain classes of contracts, subcontracts, or purchase orders (1) whenever work is to be or has been performed outside the United States and no recruitment of workers within the limits of the United States is involved; (2) for standard commercial supplies or raw materials; (3) involving less than specified amounts of money or specified numbers of workers; or (4) to the extent that they involve subcontracts below a specified tier.

(c) Section 202 of this Order shall not apply to a Government contractor or subcontractor that is a religious corporation, association, educational institution, or society, with respect to the employment of individuals of a particular religion to perform work connected with the carrying on by such corporation, association, educational institution, or society of its activities. Such contractors and subcontractors are not exempted or excused from complying with the other requirements contained in this Order.

(d) The Secretary of Labor may also provide, by rule, regulation, or order, for the exemption of facilities of a contractor that are in all respects separate and distinct from activities of the contractor related to the performance of the contract: provided, that such an exemption will not interfere with or impede the effectuation of the purposes of this Order: and provided further, that in the absence of such an exemption all facilities shall be covered by the provisions of this Order."

SEC. 5. GENERAL PROVISIONS -

(a) This order supplements but does not supersede the requirements contained in Executive Orders 13198 and 13199 of January 29, 2001.

(b) The agencies shall coordinate with the White House OFBCI concerning the implementation of this order.

(c) Nothing in this order shall be construed to require an agency to take any action that would impair the conduct of foreign affairs or the national security.

SEC. 6. RESPONSIBILITIES OF EXECUTIVE DEPARTMENTS AND AGENCIES -

All executive departments and agencies (agencies) shall:

(a) designate an agency employee to serve as the liaison and point of contact with the White House OFBCI; and

(b) cooperate with the White House OFBCI and provide such information, support, and assistance to the White House OFBCI as it may request, to the extent permitted by law.

SEC. 7. JUDICIAL REVIEW -

This order is intended only to improve the internal management of the executive branch, and it is not intended to, and does not, create any right or benefit, substantive or procedural, enforceable at law or in equity by a party against the United States, its agencies, or entities, its officers, employees or agents, or any person.

Appendix 7.
Department of Justice Equal Treatment Regulations (Excerpts)

Participation in Justice Department Programs by Religious Organizations; Providing for Equal Treatment of All Justice Department Program Participants, 69 Fed. Reg. 2832 (Jan. 21, 2004). Final Rule. Excerpts.

Department of Justice, Office of the Attorney General
Effective Date: February 20, 2004.

SUMMARY: This final rule implements executive branch policy that, within the framework of constitutional church-state guidelines, religiously affiliated (or "faith-based") organizations should be able to compete on an equal footing with other organizations for the Department's funding. It revises Department regulations to remove barriers to the participation of faith-based organizations in Department programs and to ensure that these programs are implemented in a manner consistent with the requirements of the Constitution, including the Religion Clauses of the First Amendment.

. . . .

SUPPLEMENTARY INFORMATION

I. BACKGROUND—THE SEPTEMBER 30, 2003 PROPOSED RULE

. . . .

The objective of the proposed rule was to ensure that these offices—and in particular the discretionary grants, formula grants, contracts, cooperative agreements, and other assistance administered through them—were open to all qualified organizations, regardless of their religious character, and to establish clearly the proper uses to which funds could be put and the conditions for receipt of funding. In addition, this proposed rule was designed to ensure that the implementation of the Department's programs would be conducted in a manner consistent with the requirements of the Constitution, including the Religion Clauses of the First Amendment. The proposed rule had the following specific objectives:

1. Participation by faith-based organizations in Justice Department

programs. The proposed rule provided that organizations would be eligible to participate in Department programs without regard to their religious character or affiliation, and that organizations could not be excluded from the competition for Department funds simply because they were religious. Specifically, religious organizations would be eligible to compete for funding on the same basis, and under the same eligibility requirements, as all other nonprofit organizations. The Department, as well as State and local governments administering funds under Department programs, would be prohibited from discriminating against organizations on the basis of religion, religious belief, or religious character in the administration or distribution of Federal financial assistance, including grants, contracts, and cooperative agreements.

. . . .

3. Independence of faith-based organizations. The proposed rule also clarified that a religious organization that participated in Department programs would retain its independence and could continue to carry out its mission, including the definition, practice, and expression of its religious beliefs, provided that it did not use direct financial assistance from the Department to support any inherently religious activities, such as worship, religious instruction, or proselytization. Among other things, a faith-based organization could use space in its facilities to provide Department-funded services without removing religious art, icons, scriptures, or other religious symbols. In addition, a Department-funded religious organization could retain religious terms in its organization's name, select its board members and otherwise govern itself on a religious basis, and include religious references in its organization's mission statements and other governing documents.

. . . .

5. Assurance requirements . . . In addition, to the extent that provisions of the Department's agreements, covenants, policies, or regulations disqualify religious organizations from participating in the Department's programs because they are motivated or influenced by religious faith to provide government-funded services, or because of their religious character or affiliation, the

proposed rule would remove that restriction, which is inconsistent with governing law.

II. DISCUSSION OF COMMENTS RECEIVED ON THE PROPOSED RULE

. . . .

APPLICABILITY OF THE RULE TO "COMMINGLED" FUNDS

Another commenter noted that the term "voluntarily contributes" as used in Sec. 38.1(h) may lead to confusion over the applicability of the section to commingled State and local funds. Section 38.1(h) states that "[i]f a State or local government voluntarily contributes its own funds to supplement activities carried out under the applicable programs, . . . the provisions of this section shall apply" to all of the funds that it commingles with Federal funds. The commenter suggested that the paragraph specifically include reference to "matching funds" instead of using the term "voluntarily contributed" to make it clear that the section shall apply to all funds commingled with Federal funds.

The Department believes that this section of the rule is sufficiently clear. As the rule states, when States and local governments have the option to commingle their funds with Federal funds or to separate State and local funds from Federal funds, Federal rules apply if they choose to commingle their own funds with Federal funds. Some Department programs explicitly require that Federal rules apply to State "matching" funds, "maintenance of effort" funds, or other grantee contributions that are commingled with Federal funds—i.e., are part of the grant budget. In these circumstances, Federal rules of course remain applicable to both the Federal and State or local funds that implement the program.

Another commenter stated that under the proposed rule, a State or local government has the option to segregate the Federal funds or commingle them. The commenter requested that the Department mandate that State and local funds should be kept separate from any Federal funds. Other commenters claimed, however, that the proposed rule is unclear whether it applies to State funds, or whether States can segregate their funds from Federal funds. The commenters requested that the Department revise the proposed rule to clarify the application of Federal rules to State funds.

THE FREEDOM OF FAITH-BASED ORGANIZATIONS TO STAFF ON A RELIGIOUS BASIS

The Department disagrees with these comments. As an initial matter, the Department believes it would be inappropriate to require States and local governments to separate their own funds from Federal funds circumstances where there is no matching requirement or other required grantee contribution. Where no matching requirement or other required grantee contribution is applicable, whether to commingle State and Federal funds is a decision for the States and local governments to make. In addition, for the same reasons that language concerning voluntarily commingled funds does not require clarification, the Department believes the rule requires no clarification as to whether it applies to State funds. As explained above, when States and local governments have the option to commingle their funds with Federal funds or to separate State and local funds from Federal funds, Federal rules apply only if they choose to commingle their own funds with Federal funds. Where a Department program explicitly requires that Federal rules apply to State "matching" funds, "maintenance of effort" funds, or other grantee contributions that are commingled with Federal funds—i.e., are part of the grant budget—Federal rules remain applicable to both the Federal and State or local funds that implement the program.

. . . .

APPLICABILITY AND NOTICE OF NONDISCRIMINATION REQUIREMENTS

Two commenters suggested that the Department cannot simply refer grantees to appropriate Department program offices to determine the scope of applicable independent statutory provisions requiring all grantees to agree not to discriminate in employment on the basis of religion.

The Department understands that grantees need to be aware of such provisions and believes such information is most easily obtained and best explained by the appropriate Department offices. The purpose of this rulemaking is to eliminate undue administrative barriers that the Department has imposed to the participation of faith-based organizations in Department programs; it is not to alter existing statutory requirements, which apply to Department programs to the same extent that they applied under the prior rule.

STATE AND LOCAL DIVERSITY REQUIREMENTS AND PREEMPTION

Additional comments expressed concern that the proposed rule will exempt religious organizations from State and local diversity requirements. Further, the commenters suggested that the proposed rule be modified to state that State and local laws will not be preempted by the rule.

The requirements that govern funding under the Department programs at issue in these regulations do not address preemption of State or local laws. Federal funds, however, carry Federal requirements. No organization is required to apply for funding under these programs, but organizations that apply and are selected for funding must comply with the requirements applicable to the program funds.

. . . .

RELIGIOUS FREEDOM RESTORATION ACT

Another commenter requested that the Department include language in the regulation by way of notice that the Religious Freedom Restoration Act (RFRA), 42 U.S.C. 2000bb et seq., may also provide relief from otherwise applicable provisions prohibiting employment discrimination on the basis of religion. The commenter noted that, for example, the Department of Health and Human Services has recognized RFRA's ability to provide relief from certain employment nondiscrimination requirements in the final regulations it promulgated governing its substance abuse and mental health programs.

The Department notes that RFRA, which applies to all Federal law and its implementation, 42 U.S.C. 4000bb-3, 4000bb-2(1), is applicable regardless of whether it is specifically mentioned in these regulations. Whether or not a party is entitled to an exemption or other relief under RFRA simply depends upon whether the party satisfies the requirements of that statute. The Department therefore declines to adopt this recommendation at this time.

RECOGNITION OF RELIGIOUS ORGANIZATIONS' TITLE VII EXEMPTION

A number of commenters expressed views on the rule's provision that religious organizations do not forfeit their Title VII exemption by receiving Department funds, absent statutory authority to the contrary. Some expressed appreciation that a religious organization will retain its independence in this regard, while others disagreed with the provision retaining the Title VII exemption. Some argued that it is unconstitutional for the government to provide funding for provision of social services to an organization that considers religion in its employment decisions. Others argued that Congress must expressly preserve religious organizations' Title VII exemptions—as it has done in certain welfare reform and substance abuse programs—for such organizations that receive Federal funds to retain those exemptions, and in any event that it is unwise and unfair to secular organizations to preserve such religious exemptions as a matter of executive branch policy. These commenters requested that the proposed rule be amended to provide that discrimination on the basis of religion with respect to an employment position is not allowed if an organization is federally funded.

The Department disagrees with these objections to the rule's recognition that a religious organization does not forfeit its Title VII exemption when administering Department-funded services. As an initial matter, applicable statutory nondiscrimination requirements are not altered by this rule. Congress establishes the conditions under which religious organizations are exempt from Title VII; this rule simply recognizes that these requirements, including their limitations, are fully applicable to federally funded organizations unless Congress says otherwise. As to the suggestion that the Constitution restricts the government from providing funding for social services to religious organizations that consider faith in hiring, that view does not accurately represent the law. As noted above, the employment decisions of organizations that receive extensive public funding are not attributable to the State, see *Rendell-Baker v. Kohn*, 457 U.S. 830 (1982), and it has been settled for more than 100 years that the Establishment Clause does not bar the provision of direct Federal grants to organizations that are controlled and operated exclusively by members of a single faith. See *Bradfield v. Roberts*, 175 U.S. 291 (1899); see also *Bowen v. Kendrick*, 487 U.S. 589, 609 (1988). Finally, the Department notes that allowing religious groups to consider faith in hiring when they receive government funds is much like allowing a federally funded environmental organization to hire those who share its views on protecting the environment—both groups are allowed to consider ideology and mission, which improves their effectiveness and preserves their integrity. Thus, the Department declines to amend the final rule to require religious organizations to forfeit their Title VII rights.

DISCRIMINATION ON THE BASIS OF SEXUAL ORIENTATION

One comment objected to the ability of religious organizations to discriminate on the basis of sexual orientation.

Although Federal law prohibits persons from being excluded from participation in Department services or subjected to discrimination based on race, color, national origin, sex, age, or disability, it does not prohibit discrimination on the basis of sexual orientation. We decline to impose additional restrictions by regulation.

. . . .

PART 38. EQUAL TREATMENT FOR FAITH-BASED ORGANIZATIONS

Sec. 38.1. Discretionary grants, contracts, and cooperative agreements.

Sec. 38.2. Formula grants.

. . . .

SEC. 38.1. DISCRETIONARY GRANTS, CONTRACTS, AND COOPERATIVE AGREEMENTS

(a) Religious organizations are eligible, on the same basis as any other organization, to participate in any Department program for which they are otherwise eligible. Neither the Department nor any State or local government receiving funds under any Department program shall, in the selection of service providers, discriminate for or against an organization on the basis of the organization's religious character or affiliation. As used in this section, "program" refers to a grant, contract, or cooperative agreement funded by a discretionary grant from the Department. As used in this section, the term "grantee" includes a recipient of a grant, a signatory to a cooperative agreement, or a contracting party.

. . . .

(c) A religious organization that participates in the Department-funded programs or services will retain its independence from Federal, State, and local governments, and may continue to carry out its mission, including the definition, practice, and expression of its religious beliefs, provided that it does not use direct financial assistance from the Department to support any inherently religious activities, such as worship, religious instruction, or proselytization. Among other things, a faith-based organization that receives financial assistance from the Department may use space in its facilities, without removing religious art, icons, scriptures, or other religious symbols. In addition, a religious organization that receives financial assistance from the Department retains its authority over its internal governance, and it may retain religious terms in its organization's name, select its board members on a religious basis, and include religious references in its organization's mission statements and other governing documents.

. . . .

(e) No grant document, agreement, covenant, memorandum of understanding, policy, or regulation that is used by the Department or a State or local government in administering financial assistance from the Department shall require only religious organizations to provide assurances that they will not use monies or property for inherently religious activities. Any such restrictions shall apply equally to religious and non-religious organizations. All organizations that participate in Department programs, including religious ones, must carry out eligible activities in accordance with all program requirements and other applicable requirements governing the conduct of Department-funded activities, including those prohibiting the use of direct financial assistance from the Department to engage in inherently religious activities. No grant document, agreement, covenant, memorandum of understanding, policy, or regulation that is used by the Department or a State or local government in administering financial assistance from the Department shall disqualify religious organizations from participating in the Department's programs because such organizations are motivated or influenced by religious faith to provide social services, or because of their religious character or affiliation.

(f) Exemption from Title VII employment discrimination requirements. A religious organization's exemption from the Federal prohibition on employment discrimination on the basis of religion, set forth in section 702(a) of the Civil Rights Act of 1964, 42 U.S.C. 2000e-1, is not forfeited when the organization receives direct or indirect financial assistance from the Department. Some Department programs, however, contain independent statutory provisions requiring that all grantees agree not to discriminate in employment on the basis of religion. Accordingly, grantees should consult with the appropriate Department program office to determine the scope of any applicable requirements.

. . . .

(h) Effect on State and local funds. If a State or local government voluntarily contributes its own funds to supplement activities carried out under the applicable programs, the State or local government has the option to separate out the Federal funds or commingle them. If the funds are commingled, the provisions of this section shall apply to all of the commingled funds in the same manner, and to the same extent, as the provisions apply to the Federal funds.

. . . .

SEC. 38.2. FORMULA GRANTS

(a) Religious organizations are eligible, on the same basis as any other organization, to participate in any Department program for which they are otherwise eligible. Neither the Department nor any State or local government receiving funds under any Department program shall, in the selection of service providers, discriminate for or against an organization on the basis of the organization's religious character or affiliation. As used in this section, "program" refers to a grant, contract, or cooperative agreement funded by a formula or block grant from the Department. As used in this section, the term "grantee" includes a recipient of a grant, a signatory to a cooperative agreement, or a contracting party.

. . . .

(c) A religious organization that participates in the Department-funded programs or services will retain its independence from Federal, State, and local governments, and may continue to carry out its mission, including the definition, practice, and expression of its religious beliefs, provided that it does not use direct financial assistance from the Department to support any inherently religious activities, such as worship, religious instruction, or proselytization. Among other things, a faith-based organization that receives financial assistance from the Department may use space in its facilities, without removing religious art, icons, scriptures, or other religious symbols. In addition, a religious organization that receives financial assistance from the Department retains its authority over its internal governance, and it may retain religious terms in its organization's name, select its board members on a religious basis, and include religious references in its organization's mission statements and other governing documents.

. . . .

(e) No grant document, agreement, covenant, memorandum of understanding, policy, or regulation that is used by the Department or a State or local government in administering financial assistance from the Department shall require only religious organizations to provide assurances that they will not use monies or property for inherently religious activities. Any such restrictions shall apply equally to religious and non-religious organizations. All organizations that participate in Department programs, including religious ones, must carry out eligible activities in accordance with all program requirements and other applicable requirements governing the conduct of Department-funded activities, including those prohibiting the use of direct financial assistance to engage in inherently religious activities. No grant document, agreement, covenant, memorandum of understanding, policy, or regulation that is used by the Department or a State or local government in administering financial assistance from the Department shall disqualify religious organizations from participating in the Department's programs because such organizations are motivated or influenced by religious faith to provide social services, or because of their religious character or affiliation.

(f) Exemption from Title VII employment discrimination requirements. A religious organization's exemption from the Federal prohibition on employment discrimination on the basis of religion, set forth in section 702(a) of the Civil Rights Act of 1964, 42 U.S.C. 2000e-1, is not forfeited when the religious organization receives direct or indirect financial assistance from Department. Some Department programs, however, contain independent statutory provisions requiring that all grantees agree not to discriminate in employment on the basis of religion. Accordingly, grantees should consult with the appropriate Department program office to determine the scope of any applicable requirements.

. . . .

(h) Effect on State and local funds. If a State or local government voluntarily contributes its own funds to supplement activities carried out under the applicable programs, the State or local government has the option to separate out the Federal funds or commingle them. If the funds are commingled, the provisions of this section shall apply to all of the commingled funds in the same manner, and to the same extent, as the provisions apply to the Federal funds.

. . . .

Appendix 8.
White House Policy Statement on Faith-Based Staffing

White House Office of Faith-Based and Community Initiatives, Executive Office of the President, *Protecting the Civil Rights and Religious Liberty of Faith-Based Organizations: Why Religious Hiring Must Be Preserved* (released June 23, 2003). Text and footnotes.

EXECUTIVE SUMMARY

For nearly forty years, the Civil Rights Act of 1964 has respected the right of religious groups to make religiously based employment decisions. Title VII of this Act—which is supported by Republicans and Democrats alike—protects Americans from employment discrimination based on race, color, religion, sex, and national origin. It also protects the ability of faith-based organizations to maintain their religious liberty and identity by hiring employees who share their religious beliefs.

President Bush believes that—regardless of whether government funds are involved—faith-based groups should retain their fundamental civil rights, including their Title VII right to take their faith into account when they make employment decisions.

Congress has enacted a number of additional civil rights provisions that apply to some Federal social service programs. With respect to religious hiring rights, these laws are confusing, and in some cases, contradictory. Some laws protect the hiring rights of faith-based groups that receive Federal funds, and others do not. There are now at least five different—and often conflicting—approaches that Congress has applied to religious organizations that receive a Federal grant. States and localities may have additional rules.

This hodgepodge of conflicting approaches has led to confusion for providers of social services, and a consequent reluctance by many faith-based groups to seek support from Federally funded programs. A faith-based organization that receives Federal funds to house the homeless, help them find work, and provide them with drug treatment and counseling could be subject to different Federal, State, or local rules on whether it can hire according to its religious beliefs.

It is simply too difficult and costly for many faith-based organizations to navigate these uncertain regulatory waters. The real losers are the homeless, the addicted, and others who are denied access to a range of effective social service providers, including faith-based providers.

President Bush believes in a commonsense and fair approach when faith-based organizations partner with the Federal government to provide social services. He believes faith-based organizations that receive Federal money should follow three key principles:

- They should not discriminate against any persons receiving a public service or make participation in religious activities a condition for receiving such services;

- They should be accountable for the public funds they receive and use them only for their intended purposes, with no Federal dollars being used to support inherently religious activities; and

- When they receive Federal funds, they should retain their right to hire those individuals who are best able to further their organizations' goals and mission.

At the President's direction, the Federal government has already taken many steps to put the first two of these principles into practice.

To implement the third principle, the President will work to safeguard the religious liberty of faith-based organizations that partner with the Federal government, so that they may respond with compassion to those in need in our country. He will work to preserve the Title VII rights of organizations that receive government funds. He will support changes to laws that currently prevent religious organizations that participate in these programs from taking religion into account when hiring.

Protecting the Civil Rights and Religious Liberty of Faith-Based Organizations: Why Religious Hiring Rights Must Be Preserved

Background

President Bush signed an Executive Order on December 12, 2002, seeking to end discrimination against faith-based organizations. He believes there is a moral urgency to give Americans in need the best services available, from treatment programs for addicts, to housing for the homeless, to job training for those on welfare. The full involvement of the faith community is essential to mobilize America's "armies of compassion." Successful partnerships already exist between the Federal government and many faith-based organizations, such as Lutheran Social Services, Catholic Charities, the Salvation Army, and the Jewish Federations, among others. The President seeks to build on and expand these collaborations.

A frequently asked question about President Bush's Faith-Based and Community Initiative is whether the religious organizations that receive Federal funds may take their faith into account in making employment decisions. For nearly forty years, America's landmark civil rights law has respected the right of religious groups to make religiously based employment decisions under the authority of Title VII of the Civil Rights Act of 1964. This Act protects Americans from employment discrimination based on race, color, religion, sex, and national origin.[1] At the same time, the statute also protects the ability of faith-based organizations to maintain their religious liberty and identity by hiring employees who share their religious beliefs.

To do this, the Civil Rights Act created a special exemption for religious groups, which allows them to maintain their religious identity and hire individuals supportive of their mission and vision without running afoul of the Civil Rights Act. In 1972 Congress expanded this exemption to cover all positions offered by a faith-based employer (as opposed simply to positions directly related to their ministries), and in 1987 the United States

---

[1] Additional statutes may also protect against other types of employment discrimination, such as the Age Discrimination in Employment Act of 1967 and the Americans with Disabilities Act of 1990.

Supreme Court unanimously upheld this special protection. So for more than three decades, Title VII has permitted Jewish organizations to hire only Jewish employees, Catholic organizations to hire only Catholics, and people of faith generally to hire likeminded co-religionists. As Justice Brennan wrote in upholding this law, "[d]etermining that certain activities are in furtherance of an organization's religious mission, and that only those committed to that mission should conduct them, is . . . a means by which a religious community defines itself." Title VII has thus helped protect the civil rights of people of faith.

Although many faith-based groups have flexible employment practices and have voluntarily chosen to hire both adherents and non-adherents, other religious organizations rely on the Title VII exemption in making employment decisions. The past forty years have seen no concerted effort to repeal this civil rights protection. Far from any great outcry accusing religious groups of "discriminating" in hiring, there has been nothing but support—from Republicans and Democrats alike—for this established law allowing faith-based organizations to further their purpose and vision through the people they hire.

WHAT HAPPENS WHEN A FAITH-BASED ORGANIZATION RECEIVES FEDERAL FUNDS?

What has come into question during the past decade, however, is a different issue—whether the Title VII exemption continues to apply when a religious organization receives government funds, either directly from the Federal government or from a State or locality through a block grant.

President Bush believes that—regardless of whether government funds are involved—faith-based groups should retain their fundamental civil rights, including their ability, protected under Title VII, to take their faith into account when they make employment decisions. As the Civil Rights Act of 1964 recognizes, for a faith-based organization to define or carry out its mission, it must be able to choose its employees based on its unique vision and beliefs. Such a right is rooted in the values of religious pluralism on which our nation was founded. At the same time, the President opposes using direct government funds for proselytizing and believes no recipient of a service that is supported with such funds should be forced to pray as a condition to receive that service.

Some might argue that allowing Federally funded religious groups to hire like-minded individuals is an unfair form of special treatment. But in fact this right—an organization's ability to select employees that share its common values and sense of purpose—is vital to all organizations, not just faith-based groups. A secular group that receives government money is currently free to hire based on its ideology and mission. Allowing religious groups to consider faith in hiring when they receive government funds simply levels the playing field—by making sure that, when it comes to serving impoverished Americans, faith-based groups are as welcome at the government's table as non-religious ones.

Imagine the reaction of the World Wildlife Fund—which has received more than $115 million in Federal support since 1996—if it were required to hire employees without regard to their position on environmental conservation. Or that of Planned Parenthood—the recipient of millions of Federal dollars each year—if it had to hire staff without considering their views on abortion or birth control. Some people agree with the missions of these organizations, others do not. But no one can deny that these organizations' ability to execute their goals hinges on whether they may choose to hire like-minded people.

That is why President Bush believes that the right of all organizations—including faith-based groups—to keep their identity when they receive Federal funds should be a straightforward proposition. But in the past several decades, Congress has enacted a number of civil rights provisions that apply to Federal social service programs. The problem is that, with respect to religious hiring rights, these laws are confusing, and in some cases, contradictory. Some laws protect the hiring rights of faith-based groups that receive Federal funds, and others do not. In fact, as described below, there are now at least five different—and often conflicting—approaches that Congress has applied to religious organizations that receive a Federal grant.

To make matters even more complicated, a number of States and localities have statutes, regulations, and ordinances that contain express language prohibiting discrimination on the basis of religion and/or sexual orientation. Most of these laws exempt religious organizations that receive government funds, but some do not.

CONGRESS'S FIVE DIFFERENT APPROACHES TO RELIGIOUS HIRING

- **No special rules.** Many programs have no special civil rights rules. These are the so-called "silent statutes." An example of such a law is the Older Americans Act, which funds many important programs for elders in need. If a statute authorizing Federal funds contains no additional civil rights language, then the background rules of the Civil Rights Act—including the religious hiring exemption for religious employers—apply. Thus, an organization that receives funds from this type of program may continue to take its faith into account in making employment decisions without running into problems with Title VII—just as it did before receiving a grant.

  Numerous courts have recognized that religious organizations that receive Federal financial assistance retain their exemption under the Civil Rights Act of 1964 to hire on a religious basis.[2]

- **Charitable Choice rules.** The Charitable Choice statutes apply to the Department of Health and Human Services' (HHS) Temporary Assistance to Needy Families (TANF) and Community Services Block Grant (CSBG) programs, as well as to programs administered by the Substance Abuse and Mental Health Services Administration (SAMHSA). These statutes expressly protect a religious organization's Title VII exemption even if it is Federally funded. Thus, just as for programs governed by "silent statutes," organizations that receive funds from the Charitable Choice programs can continue to take their faith into account in making employment decisions, without running into problems with Title VII. Nor are they subject to any additional hiring restrictions.[3] In

---

[2] *See Hall v. Baptist Memorial Health Care Corp.,* 215 F.3d 618 (6th Cir. 2000); *Siegel v. Truett-McConnell College,* 13 F. Supp. 1335 (N.D. Ga. 1994), *aff'd,* 73 F.3d 1108 (11th Cir. 1995); *Young v. Shawnee Mission Med. Center,* 1988 U.S. Dist. Lexis 12248, at 4-5 (D. Kan. 1988); *see also Pedreira v. Kentucky Baptist Home for Children,* 186 F. Supp. 2d 757 (W.D. Ky 2001).

[3] The one exception is the SAMHSA block grant programs, which are subject to an additional rule, along

1996 President Clinton signed the first of four "charitable choice" laws passed by Congress thus expressly permitting faith-based organizations to hire according to their religious beliefs while receiving Federal funds. These laws have worked well and there has been no record of any adverse impact from them.

- **Three special rules.** A number of Federal assistance programs are subject to additional civil rights provisions in the laws authorizing these programs. In a sense, these provisions are an overlay or an add-on to the Title VII rules. That is, although organizations that receive funds from these programs retain their Title VII exemption, they must also comply with these other civil rights provisions, which contain no exemption for religious organizations.[4] Social service programs that contain special rules like this are of three types:

  1. Programs with additional statutory civil rights language that does not specifically mention employment, such as Community Development Block Grant (CDBG) and the Head Start programs. These statutes have language along the following lines:

     > No person shall on the ground of race, color, national origin, religion or sex be excluded from participation in, be denied the benefits of, or be subjected to discrimination under any program or activity funded in whole or in part with funds made available under this chapter.

     This statutory approach clearly protects individuals that receive Federally funded services from being denied assistance simply because they are of a different faith or no faith at all. However,

---

the lines of the first "special rule" described below. This statutory provision, which applies to sex and religious discrimination, makes clear that people who receive SAMHSA services may not be discriminated against based on sex or religion. To carry out Congress's intention in enacting the Charitable Choice laws, the Administration has proposed a rule clarifying that this statutory provision does not apply to the employment practices of religious organizations that receive funding, if it would substantially burden their exercise of religion. The proposed regulation relies on the Religious Freedom Restoration Act (RFRA), which applies to all Federal agencies. In RFRA, Congress said that Federal agencies could not substantially burden religious exercise without a compelling interest.

[4]Under all three of these special rules, however, faith-based organizations may be entitled to additional protection under the Religious Freedom Restoration Act.

some older U.S. Supreme Court cases indicate that these statutes may also apply to employment decisions. If they do, then faith-based groups may forfeit their ability to make employment decisions on a religious basis when they receive funds from these programs.

2. Programs with additional statutory civil rights language that specifically mentions employment, such as the Department of Labor's Workforce Investment Act and the Omnibus Crime and Control & Safe Streets Act. These statutes have civil rights language identical to the CDBG and Head Start laws, but they also specifically mention employment. Again, for these programs, Federally funded religious organizations may forfeit their religious hiring rights.

3. Programs with additional statutory civil rights language that specifically mention employment and also eliminate the Title VII religious hiring exemption for faith-based organizations. For these programs, Congress has made very clear its intention to prohibit faith-based organizations from taking religion into account when it hires new staff or selects program participants.

THE NEED TO PRESERVE HIRING RIGHTS FOR FAITH-BASED ORGANIZATIONS

What is the result of this patchwork quilt of conflicting approaches? Confusion for providers of social services, and a consequent reluctance by many faith-based groups to administer Federally funded programs. It is simply too difficult and costly for many faith-based organizations to navigate these uncertain regulatory waters. For example, a faith-based organization that receives Federal funds to house the homeless, help them find work, and provide them with drug treatment and counseling could be subject to different Federal, State, or local rules and regulations on whether it can hire according to its religious beliefs. In other words, this organization might be permitted to take religion into account in hiring employees that provide the drug treatment parts of its program, but not be permitted to take religion into account for those employees who help that same person in need find work. This makes absolutely no sense. Why should a single homeless shelter be subject to different—and diametrically opposing—hiring policies?

President Bush believes this tangle of laws has discouraged many effective faith-based providers from competing to provide government-funded services. The real victims of this contradictory statutory scheme are, of course, the needy Americans who could be helped by faith-based providers. The President is committed to providing these citizens with access to the most effective programs, regardless of the provider's religious affiliation or non-affiliation. He is committed to making sure that providers that receive direct Federal funds never discriminate against beneficiaries of Federally funded services on any basis, including religion, race, national origin, sex, personal views, or sexual orientation. He is committed to making sure that Federal funds are properly used, and he has instructed Federal agencies to guard zealously against the use of direct government aid to support worship or other inherently religious activities.

At the same time, he will continue to work to protect the civil rights and religious liberty of faith-based organizations that partner with the Federal government, so that they may respond with compassion to those in need in our country. As a step in this direction, on December 12, 2002, he amended Executive Order 11246 to permit faith-based organizations with Federal contracts to take their faith into account in making employment decisions, consistent with the long-established rights that faith-based organizations have enjoyed under the Civil Rights Act of 1964.[5] Religious organizations will no longer be required to forfeit their Title VII exemption in order to bid for one of these contracts. This Executive Order applies primarily to government contracts, as opposed to the billions of dollars that are awarded annually in Federal grants that are administered pursuant to Congress's direction.

President Bush will continue to work to make clear that faith-based organizations that receive Federal funds retain their civil rights to base employment decisions on their beliefs and vision. At the Federal level, this means that the Administration will support changes to laws, like the Workforce Investment Act and the Head Start statute, that currently prevent

---

[5]EO 11246 sets out a number of equal opportunity employment rules that apply to Federal contracts in excess of $10,000 and authorizes the Department of Labor to enforce its provisions. Until President Bush's action, the EO did not contain an exemption for religious groups like Section 702 of the Civil Rights Act of 1964. While no figures are available on the number of contracts affected, each year the Federal government executes over 30,000 contracts in excess of $25,000, covering a wide range of Federal services.

religious organizations that participate in these programs from taking religion into account when hiring.

With respect to States and localities, the President will urge the courts to provide guidance on whether faith-based organizations are required to comply with State and local ordinances that restrict their ability to participate in Federally funded formula and block grant programs.

CONCLUSION

Faith-based groups are an essential resource to the neediest citizens in our country. The effectiveness of these organizations comes from their commitment to serving others—a commitment that is grounded in their faith. But to remain effective, these groups must be allowed to maintain their religious identity, central to which is the ability to select employees who share their vision. Without this essential right, an organization loses its ability to promote common values, a sense of community and unity of purpose, and shared experiences through service.

President Bush will strive to ensure that faith-based organizations that receive Federal funds retain their civil right to base employment decisions on their ideals and mission. These efforts will enable Americans in need to have access to the widest array of social service providers and receive the most effective assistance available.

President Bush launched the faith-based and community initiative as "a determined attack on need" so that America's "armies of compassion" can be mobilized to feed the hungry, house the homeless, treat the addicted, and help those who despair. He remains hopeful that people of all faiths or no faith at all, as well as Democrats, Republicans and Independents alike, can unite in this effort.

Appendix 9.
Ten Affirmations on Religious Staffing

1. For over thirty years, Title VII of the Civil Rights Act of 1964, as amended, has honored the right of faith-based organizations to choose the employees who can best further their missions, by explicitly acknowledging in section 702(a) their freedom to use religious criteria when making their employment decisions.

2. This religious staffing option is not an exemption *from* the Civil Rights Act, but a *freedom incorporated into it*. Religious staffing is a civil right belonging to faith-based organizations, not a denial of civil rights. Under Title VII, religious organizations may not discriminate on the basis of sex, race, national origin, handicap, or age, but they are free to hire only staff who share their religious beliefs. Opponents of religious staffing are seeking to roll back a long-established civil right.

3. The religious staffing freedom applies to all positions in a faith-based organization, not only ministerial or clergy positions. This broad religious staffing freedom was upheld unanimously by the U.S. Supreme Court in 1987 in *Amos v. Corporation of Presiding Bishops*, a case involving the dismissal of a janitor from a faith-based health club. The Court ruled that the exemption permitting religious staffing by religious organizations was not only constitutionally permissible but fully consistent with the First Amendment.

4. Although the First Amendment has sometimes been interpreted as requiring a high wall of separation between church and state, thus forbidding funding for overtly religious organizations, the U.S. Supreme Court has decisively moved away from this interpretation in favor of a policy of treating faith-based and secular organizations on an equal basis. The religious staffing freedom is consistent with this policy and necessary to enable religious organizations to retain their religious identity when they serve in the public square.

5. In accommodating religious staffing by faith-based organizations, the Civil Rights Act only enables them to do what most other mission-driven organizations, such as the Sierra Club and Planned Parenthood, also do: choose as staff those capable people who are most dedicated to the cause of the organization.

6. If a faith-based organization accepts federal funds to provide social services, it does not on that account give up its religious staffing freedom. There is no general federal legal or constitutional principle that eliminates the religious staffing freedom of faith-based organizations that accept government money. Title VI of the Civil Rights Act, the section dealing with federally funded organizations, does not include religion as a prohibited basis of discrimination.

7. The current state of religious employment law is complex, inconsistent, and inadequate. Religious organizations are generally free to use religious criteria in employment decisions, but certain federal programs, such as those funded under the Workforce Investment Act, prohibit all grantees, including faith-based organizations, from hiring on a religious basis. However, religious organizations in such cases may appeal to the Religious Freedom Restoration Act to override the restriction, as noted in current regulations for SAMHSA drug treatment funding. Other laws for federal social service programs are silent about employment, and thus leave the general religious staffing freedom intact. During the Clinton administration, Congress added Charitable Choice language to laws authorizing four federal programs, in order explicitly to protect religious staffing for faith-based organizations funded under those programs.

8. The freedom to staff on a religious basis is not a freedom to discriminate on religious grounds against recipients of social services. Both Charitable Choice and the principles of the Bush Faith-Based and Community Initiative explicitly forbid religious discrimination against people seeking assistance.

9. Religious staffing is not "government-funded discrimination," as critics claim. If the government selects a faith-based provider, it is choosing the organization that most effectively and efficiently serves the needy, in this instance an organization that has the legal freedom to ensure that its staff members are committed to its faith-based mission.

10. The government is acting in an even-handed way when it permits all organizations it funds, religious as well as secular, to hire staff devoted to their respective missions. Pro-choice organizations do not lose their ability to screen out pro-life employees when they accept government funds. In the same way, faith-based service groups should not lose their religious staffing liberty if they accept federal grants. Keeping religious

staffing legal is the only way to ensure equal opportunity and effectiveness for all organizations and to respect the diversity of faith communities that are part of our civil society.

12.17.2003

Source: Coalition to Preserve Religious Freedom, a multi-faith coalition of faith-based social-service, higher-education, and religious freedom organizations, hosted by the Center for Public Justice.

About the Authors

Carl H. Esbeck (J.D., Cornell) holds the *R. B. Price* Professorship, and is the *Isabelle Wade and Paul C. Lyda* Professor of Law, at the University of Missouri-Columbia. During 2001 and 2002 he was Senior Counsel to the Deputy Attorney General, U.S. Department of Justice, and Director of the Task Force for Faith-Based and Community Initiatives at the Department of Justice. Esbeck is the progenitor of the legislative proposal which has come to be called Charitable Choice, and he worked with senatorial staff from 1995 through 2000 in drafting its provisions for four federal social-service programs.

Stanley W. Carlson-Thies (Ph.D., Toronto) is the Director of Social Policy Studies at the Center for Public Justice, Annapolis, Maryland. During 2001 and 2002 he served on the staff of the White House Office of Faith-Based and Community Initiatives, where he worked on legal and policy development and coordinated reviews of federal laws, regulations, and programs to identify and reform inappropriate restrictions on the participation of faith-based and community-based organizations. He is the author of *Charitable Choice for Welfare & Community Services: An Implementation Guide for State, Local, and Federal Officials* (2000) and other publications on the relationship between government and religious and secular social-service providers.

Ronald J. Sider (Ph.D., Yale) is Professor of Theology, Holistic Ministry and Public Policy and Director of the Sider Center on Ministry and Public Policy at Eastern Baptist Theological Seminary, as well as President of Evangelicals for Social Action. His *Rich Christians in an Age of Hunger* was recognized by *Christianity Today* as one of the one hundred most influential religious books of the twentieth century. Sider's most recent books are *The Scandal of the Evangelical Conscience: Why Are Christians Living Just Like the Rest of the World; Just Generosity: A New Vision for Overcoming Poverty in America;* and *Churches That Make a Difference: Reaching Your Community with Good News and Good Works* (with Phil Olson and Heidi Unruh). He serves on many advisory boards, including Pew Forum on Religion and Public Life and Faith and the Service Technical Education Network of the National Crime Prevention Council.